built environment

eindhoven university of technology

naio10 publishers, rotterdam

built environment 2013-2014

editor
jos bosman

editorial board
theo arentze
bert blocken
rijk blok
bernard colenbrander

editorial assistents
thijs de goede
mark kanters
joris pierik
marieke de vries

graphic design
jac de kok

translation
david lee
joris pierik

printer
lecturis

acknowledgements
brian mcgrath
sukanya krishnamurthy
winnie wong

photographers
bart van overbeeke
frans schellekens
willem schilte
daniël venneman
rob van wendel de joode

isbn 978-94-6208-161-1

table of contents

preface

Built Environment 13-14 presents a selection of graduation projects, doctoral and staff research from the period between September 2013 to September 2014.

Three topics represent the direction and focus of research at our department:
1. Sustainable Transformation; 2. Smart living environments; 3. Quality of life.

Colleague Jeanne Dekkers proposed to contrast the attitudinal bend one requires in working on topics of sustainable transformation with the programmatic ones of quality of life (especially health), through a succinct choice of verbs: **sense** and **care**. In an analogical sense the verbs **move** and **live** may be considered relevant for exploring specific aspects that can make the built environment smart (i.e. houses and cities). In this segment of the research investigation wishes of the customer and user is highly relevant. A third verb couple, **learn** and **make**, may be indicative of how at our department various colleagues explore the possibilities of improving the quality of materials, indoor climate quality, the logic of placing buildings in relation to wind patterns, and construction methods. It is about how buildings are both made and could possibly perform better. Building physics experiments (in the laboratory) are an essential part of this research practice.

The six verbs organized alphabetically offers an overall thematic output of our department, as presented in this yearbook.
Care = the process through which the design of buildings plays a role in translating social agendas for care into a functional built environment while considering a quality of use. Each time period has another idea and agenda for a bathroom, a prison, a hospital, the adequately designed environment for taking care of elderly people, etc.
Learn = improving the technical performance of the materials and equipment of a building.
Live = innovating and rethinking existing protocols for living.
Make = innovating and rethinking existing protocols for making.
Move = innovating and rethinking existing protocols for moving.
Sense = enlarging the sensibilities that can be experienced in the built environment.

These six verbs all at once place the work of architects, building and mechanical engineers and product designers in a dialogue of parallel research.

Designers in our research community stimulate the experiments of applied research. To mention an outstanding example presented in this book is a kinetic watertight structural system with solar panels that can track the path of the sun, the theme of the graduation project of Peter Koelewijn and Lucas Klerk. Having developed their concept by making a series of prototypes, the final design combines the practice and teaching experience of Arjan Habraken concerning lightweight constructions, the experience of Arno Pronk with materializing curvilinear membrane surfaces and the engineering practice of Patrick Teuffel. The combinatory result is a kinetic tensegrity structure with a stable membrane roof and hinging vertical struts. An amazing demonstration of interdisciplinary technology and design.

Architects like Femke Stout (in her graduation project) motivate technology designers to become more sensitive in the manner in which their products are finished. The world of the senses is of importance in relation to technological possibilities. For instance, buildings in which glass may become a structural constructive element and steel connections may consequently become extra thin (graduation project of Dennie Dierks) and where solar energy elements may become integrated in glass (graduation project of Charlotte Zhang). I'm proud that the output shows that we are excelling in becoming a school where the poetry of designers and the adventure of technological research and experiment find and influence one another. The attention the Ice Dome received earlier this year, shows the growing awareness of general public to the profile of our department, and is slowly on it's way to becoming more outspoken.

On the occasion of the yearly Dutch Design Week (DDW) in October 2014, half of the content of this book is presented as exhibition items. In the hall 2A of the Klokgebouw at Strijp S, a prime location of the DDW, the inspirational 2013-2014 output of the Built Environment Department is shown together with examples of Industrial Design and Mechanical Engineering products and research. Presenting this work at the Dutch Design Week means directing a spotlight on the types of research that were formerly somewhat hidden from public attention.

A possible conclusion to draw: the profile of research at our department has become more tangible. I am looking forward to arriving at the next level of becoming even more recognizable, the coming year.

Elphi Nelissen
Dean of the Department of the Built Environment

office of oma, 14/f on hing building, hong kong

"design follows research, engagement and understanding"

"I'm committed to outspoken architectural ideas that are bold and go beyond the usual borders of ideas or architectural styles; the architectural ideas need to be contextually relevant"

interview with david gianotten

jos bosman

The interview with David Gianotten, an alumnus of Eindhoven University of Technology, started as an exchange of emails, moved to a Skype conversation, and culminated with a meeting in Amsterdam. During this period the office structure of OMA changed: from six partners (of which Gianotten is one), to ten. Coinciding with our meeting was the first meeting of the new office partner constellation. Focused on developing a strategy for operating as an 'oiled machine', Gianotten's management talent seems to play a steadily increasing role.

After having worked in OMA's Rotterdam office for only one and a half years, he went on to set up OMA's office in Hong Kong, as a partner. Gianotten arrived in Hong Kong to take on the responsibility of the last phase of construction of the CCTV tower in Beijing, and from his moment of arrival had to match the Chinese pace of demand for building production and nosedive into delivery. He explained the change in approach, he introduced in the Hong Kong office, to Andrew Mackenzie in an interview that was published two weeks before we started our conversation: "When I first came to this office [in Rotterdam], the teams would present fifty or sixty different options (...) That, in my opinion, cannot be the starting point of a serious design process; there should be an exchange of argument, then of course the options. So in Asia, we seldom work with more than three to five options in a design process." The reason: "(...)here in Asia, when we meet with our clients, they are the top bosses, so their decision stands. (...)I am here as a partner, I have full decision powers on everything; I don't need to report back to a design board in Rotterdam for a final decision. For many clients, that's very attractive as our competitors are organized with design boards and their branch offices have limited decision-making power. With clients who are very direct here, they want to go fast, they want to say yes or no, and they expect you to do the same."

Gianotten's statement and client experience can be contrasted with those of John van de Water, another Dutchman (alumnus of Delft University of Technology) who established a branch office of Amsterdam based Next Architects in Beijing. He would come to understand Gianotten's strategy by stumbling his way for years through feng shui influences on small and medium sized buildings, and writing a book about it titled 'You cannot change China, China changes you'. In the book van de Water explains with a great sense for situation comic that the Dutch conceptual approach and arguments do not work in China.

ARCHIPRIX International director, Henk van der Veen who for many years has been following the results of different approaches between Delft and Eindhoven, summarises (in a conversation with me in Delft, September 2014): "...the Delft trained architects though manifest more ideas in their approach as designers, the Eindhoven ones are in general the better building engineers".

the interview

JB: *Which projects in practice define your search for, and grip on the reality of building, before you joined OMA in 2008?*
DG: This is a really difficult question as I was involved in many different building efforts in different roles before I joined OMA in 2008; in these different efforts I learned different skills at different scales. To choose, I would like to mention three that are very dear to me and they all mark different moments in my career, and confronted me with different dilemma's related to having grip on the reality of building. 1. The extension of my mother's house in the South of France, which is a project I did in private and is probably the smallest project I was ever involved in, but also the most personal. 2. The creation and building process of De TwentseWelle in Enschede which I did in collaboration with SeARCH and is part of the rebuilding of Roombeek. 3. The design and construction of the Favrholm project for Novo Nordisk in Denmark which I did while being a director at SeARCH.

JB: *How did you get involved in the rebuilding of Roombeek, after the traumatic fire incident in Enschede?*
DG: This was through my previous working relationship with Peter Kuenzli in Leidsche Rijn, Utrecht. Peter requested me, in his role as project director for the rebuilding, to come up with a proposal for the building of four centrally located clusters of amenities for the neighborhood. These amenities were to be programmed and designed with and for the people that lived in the neighborhood before the disaster, as well as for the new inhabitants after the rebuilding. The initial idea was created to make a place of memory for the disaster, a museum showing the unique nature and craftsmanship of Twente, a cluster of schools (brede school), and a healthcare and assisted living center. In this process I was responsible for

the creation of the brief for the projects, the selection of architects to work with (including SeARCH and OMA/Rem Koolhaas), the project management during design, the public engagement, the execution of the design and coordination with the different contractors and in the end the delivery and opening of the project. This engagement shows that I was broadly interested in the process of building and everything I could do within the realm of my profession. Importantly my training was targeted towards execution of the ideas. The fact that I collaborated with four very different architects for the projects shows that I'm also committed to outspoken architectural ideas that are bold and go beyond the usual borders of ideas or architectural styles; the architectural ideas need to be contextually relevant.

JB: *I want to come back to your attention for context later on in the interview, as have I noticed you talk about it in your lectures as well. What I first would like to expand on is this wide spectrum of experience that seems to unfold itself in this narrative, immediately and almost naturally, and without a prefixed agenda around your personal involvement in practice. This spectrum reaches from organizational matters such as briefing, to an involvement in matters of taste and the refinement of design. How did that work in for instance the Favrholm project? I saw the fantastic photographs Iwan Baan captured of them, where the interior looks like a recycled wooden frame. Akin to subtlety of rigidness..., impressive! Did the process dictate the variety of your roles in the realization of that project? And, how did the experience of making that particular project, one of your three dear ones, shape your professional attitude?*

DG: Indeed I have been widely interested in all aspects of our profession from day one, since my time at the TUE. I have always had difficulties to devote myself to design only, as after the deign process I immediately wanted to understand how I could realize the design ideas, and how I could convince the various engineers and the client that the ideas were actually possible! I thought that the best way would be to get involved in all of these processes, to understand as much as possible. So after my graduation from the TUE, to be able to understand the various decision-making processes in a project from diverse points of view, I tired to practice these different roles within a design process. In the Favrholm project I managed the competition submission of SeARCH and was also an integral part of the design team. Together with Bjarne Mastenbroek I delivered the competition design presentation and also presented our process approach document to the client in which we described how we would work together with the client, local specialists and stakeholders. We also made a proposal for modification of the original requested program based on an analysis

of Novo Nordisk as a company and their training process. This meant that our competition submission was from day one more than just a design, which the client appreciated a lot because it was the first time for them to procure a preservation / newly-built project. Through this approach we became a discussion and development partner to the client rather than just the architect. During the design stages of the project I kept fulfilling the role as a discussion partner for the client and designer within the SeARCH team. I left SeARCH just after the project was contracted out by the client and the building process started, but I kept following the building process closely from a distance and visited the project during construction and immediately after completion. In general you can say that I like to be more than an architect only. I like to be involved in as many aspects of a project as possible and understand the reasoning from all sides as well as I can. I believe that through this understanding I can be a strategic partner to the client, which gave me the possibility to work on innovative ideas and solutions and determining how they can become reality.

JB: *Also when you kept following the building process of Favrholm: was it not a very risky step to leave your leading position in this particular realization process to switch to another office where you took over the lead of an ongoing building process? How it is to have participated in a design that you did not finish as a building process (Favrholm) and to finish a building process in which you were not involved in the design (the CCTV complex)?*
DG: Apart from (one of) the projects you work on in an architectural office there are many other challenges. When you have a key position that can also determine if you can flourish in the created environment. With SeARCH, I based that on the experience with Favrholm, and I wanted more international exposure than the environment would allow. Therefore when I got the chance to become Rem Koolhaas' executive manager - architect I jumped at that opportunity. I knew that I had to leave people and projects behind that were very dear to me at SeARCH, including the Favrholm project, but at the same time I knew the project was in very good hands and this opportunity would only come once. When I started at OMA I could more or less create my own role and started working on many projects. It quickly became evident that my experience with different projects, roles and broad view related to the profession came in hand, including the CCTV and SZSE projects. Over time my role in different projects within OMA grew including, and many of them were located in Asia, therefore in a very natural way I took on the further business development on that continent for OMA. It was not hard for me to take on projects that had already been started in that process, although my role only became

publically more apparent when Ole Scheeren left and I became part of the OMA Partnership. It is also important to mention that for me it was already clear that when I started my study at the TUE that without taking any risk in the architectural profession it will be hard to grow to a position quickly in which you can lead, build and go after your ultimate ambitions. Therefore I have never been afraid of taking risky decisions and taking a less conventional route to end up where I wanted to be, even when that meant I could not finish something that was dear to me.

JB: *How is it possible that even as a student you were aware that you wanted to take a non-traditional route for being successful in practice, than that of the architect who conquers the world because of his ideas? What did the TUE offer you as an environment in the first year that convinced you of such an option? Did you get the impression that more students thought like you; did you have allies? Was there chemistry between you and teachers?*
DG: I think it was mainly based on intuition. I saw many people starting their education by choosing one singular direction as defined by the offered curriculum, while I was not willing and ready to choose for one direction. When I asked the TUE staff if I could keep doing elements from different subject areas, the TUE was very accommodating. This made following multiple routes easier and that felt good to me. I kept doing this during my education and afterwards when I started work. I guess it fits me best if I can find my own way to achieve what I believe is the best. As I didn't live in Eindhoven I didn't have many allies amongst the students. However from many tutors I received much support; teachers like [Huub] Smulders, [Jan Thijs] Boekholt, [Jan] Westra, and [Wim] Schaefer helped me to explore my own path.

JB: *Did the chair of architectural history and theory have no appeal to you? During the time you studied at TUE, this chair was promoted as an idea of an Eindhoven School of architects., Joost Ector, looking back on his period of study wrote an essay in 1999 about the 'Eindhoven School' of the 1990's. He points at two particular influences: 1. the lectures of Pieter-Jan Gijsberts on Adolf Loos, and 2. Rem Koolhaas as "phantom teacher" - "Despite his physical absence, Koolhaas is able to passively become more important than any other teacher, including those who are present. Koolhaas as the 'phantom-teacher' is, in all his absence, more prominent than any other at the foundation of the 'Eindhoven School'." Isn't that funny? Were you aware, at the time you studied, of these 'mythological proportions' of the influence of Loos and Rem? Or were these impressions roaming around in a corner of the faculty that escaped your attention?*
DG: I'm not aware of the Joost Ector's essay about the 'Eindhoven School' of the 1990's. But I am aware of the influential lectures about Adolf Loos and Le Corbusier given by Pieter-Jan Gijsberts. Though I was influenced by the discussion about the Raumplan, my attention was very quickly diverted to architects working 30 years prior to me starting architectural school and at that moment in Japan and Scandinavia. In other words the lectures and discussions were fascinating and the content shaped how I looked at architecture, but I was more interested in more contemporary architects at that time. Strangely enough I didn't notice much of the influence of Rem Koolhaas on the education in Eindhoven at that time, maybe because it was physically absent and therefore unspoken. In my opinion OMA's work and Rem Koolhaas his writing was studied carefully, but alongside the work of many other influential architects of the 20th century, and therefore in an elaborate context. It can however well be that because of my broad approach to project work and me not living in Eindhoven I didn't fully participate in the purely architectural debate that was happening amongst the students; in this case me following my own route might have made me miss out on a part of the debate that might have been there. However, being at OMA now for 6 years has made me catch up for sure!

JB: *(laughs): Indeed. In the meantime you participated actively in questioning the stereotypical opinions and reframing concerns when it comes to the influence of Rem Koolhaas/OMA on the debate. One is about the relevance of 'context', a typical concern of the Cornell school where Rem once studied. According to the stereotypical opinion, Favrholm is a 100% contextual example and CCTV a 100% anti-contextual one. In your own observations – that I saw in a recorded lecture - various buildings of OMA that according to stereotypical opinion are anti-contextual, are in fact part of created urban contexts. But staying within the comparison of the two examples of our conversation, a completely opposite attitude is apparent, isn't it? Almost one that with all your capacities to relate to different architectural attitudes, must have worked as a schizophrenic effect on the moment you switched from SeARCH to OMA. However in the Shenzhen Stock Exchange Building in Shenzhen and Taipei Performing Arts Centre in Taiwan an attitude of what you consider to be a contemporary type of contextual attitude is realized. Can you explain that, also within the perspective of a personal experience, as I just sketched?*
DG: To be honest the switch from SeARCH to OMA went rather seamlessly, and didn't provoke a big change in my approach to architecture and didn't require a personality shift. I think that most work of OMA is contextual and is embedded in both the intellectual and physical context of the assignment. In most cases the context is well detailed and an extensive research is carried out on the project,

which then shapes the design decisions. Personally this design approach to any complex situation fits my personal approach very well. Also the freedom I received within OMA to experiment with the OMA design approach to make it my own and to infuse it with my thoughts and ideas related to the conception of projects was large. This made that after a few weeks I felt very much at home at OMA and received a lot of responsibility without having a long history within the company. If you look at the work we do in Asia at the moment you can probably recognize this context infused design approach, hence your questions about TPAC and the Shenzhen Stock Exchange Building. The fact that you recognize this is for me a compliment in itself because it shows that it is visible that OMA uses more of a process to design than a prescribed style, and that there is space for personal influence at all design levels of the organization which marks the constant development of the office and its work; I find this personally very important.

JB: Form follows process? Let me resume what I understand of your design strategy. It has become more clear to me in our conversation that though Loos and Le Corbusier were a common ground for architectural design exercises at the time when you were studying, your own path - of combining the basics of these common aspirations with the knowledge of other disciplines - defined your toolbox for design. In many ways making your study experience relevant for later practice. As far as personal orientation, you mentioned Scandinavia and Japan. Was Itsuko Hasegawa a special reference for you, already as a student? I had to think of his work immediately, the first time seeing your design for the Taipei Performing Arts Centre... Or do you find me a persistent academic, when I try to find at least one personal reference behind the doubtlessly complex processes, in which many specialists and designers are involved, and that you manage from Hong Kong?
DG: Rather 'Design follows Research, Engagement and Understanding'. I don't mind you insisting to get a personal reference from me, however it is hard to name one or two specifically. My mind works very visually and constantly maps elements of many different references and puts them into inspiration, not solutions, for specific design engagements. In other words, references in my mind are very often virtual and fictional, mapped out of many different images that constantly flick through my head while thinking of a design challenge. This image bank contains images of buildings from well-known and anonymous architects I have seen in reality, publications, and films, some are even created out of words I read or heard. However if you would like me to mention a personal reference of an architect from Japan I'm inspired by in particular, I have read a lot about, tried to get close to and interacted with over the years than

I mention Arata Isozaki. In the last few years I had the honor to collaborate with him, present next to him and compete against him (with different degrees of success).

JB: Being able to compete with Isozaki, or with any other famous Japanese architect, implies being able to represent (and convey) in more than just ideas and images. But it is long stretch between representing an idea to being able to control a process to careful realization. The finished Shenzhen Stock Exchange Building for example looks to have been carried out with a type of precision one can relate to the Japanese or the Swiss. How did you and your team manage to reach this quality?
DG: To be able to reach the quality one sees in the Shenzhen Stock Exchange we had to operate very strategically during all design stages of the project, and even more importantly during the execution phases of the project. In the design stages we strategically chose which architectural design concepts to introduce to the building and decided to stick to just a few; the lifted large plan podium, the integration of the data center on site, the podium roof park, and the lobbies with their skylights. Secondly, we decided to only work with a limited amount of materials and a limited amount of details, in this way, during construction patch works of materials and inferior detail execution China is so famous for, could be avoided. And then during the execution phases we had an architectural team on the site at all times that the contractors and sub-contractors were having people building on the site. Us and the various contractors were asked to mock up the main project design elements on site, and perfected the execution method within all details, before they were executed in the building. This collaboration and 'testing' process lead to a building with a quality level that is far beyond the usual Chinese execution level; I find it a compliment that you compare it to the Japanese and Swiss standard, because that is obviously what we aimed for, with the ambition to show the rest of the world that with a careful and well thought of process this is possible anywhere, including China.

JB: In an interview with Crane.tv, you mentioned you always have some glue with you when you travel, for potentially adopting or repairing the little models you carry around with you of the big buildings you are planning to realize. Most of them look like gadgets that already have a lot of character, and speak about the ambition to become realized in the refined way we just discussed. Can you tell a bit more about the smallness and the aura of refinedness of these models? Are they comparable to toys for the top bosses who ultimately make the decision?
DG: These small models give me the possibility to touch and visualize the building and its surrounding

and interior spaces better. They also help me to think of improvements in the 3D sense; while working on a design concept I always go through physical modifications and the models are a tool to make that possible. I use small models out of practicality, they travel with me, and because they don't have the amount of detail you can get lost in. In other words: They don't show the tactility of the buildings themselves even though they are quite refined; they represent the 3D or physical diagram. There is no aura to the models other than the importance they have during the design process, I also never use them in presentations or in dialogue with clients, they are made and modified for and by me to go through a for me necessary process.

JB: *My last question is if you have any recommendations for the current students of architecture, building technology, building physics, construction design, construction management and urban design at the TUE? How can they profit from the offered education format, which still - like in the period you studied - allows for interdisciplinary research and design? In fact the new bachelor and master program intends to enlarge the scope of possibilities even further. Apart from attending stimulating lectures from other departments (besides the ones from the building environment), the master students from next year will have the option to go for half a year for practice or study abroad. The most difficult thing for most students seems to be the choice of possible experiences so that they end up with a useful toolbox for practice. Their worry is often: what to combine? What is a strong combination of experiences? What can you advise them? For optimizing their career perspective...*

DG: The most important advice I can give them is to make their study a fun time, not only in the café but also at the university. It is a time in which you can explore; can make choices that turn out right and that sometimes turn out wrong, but in that event then just turn a different corner the next time. There is no magic formula of combining certain elements, the most important is to look beyond the borders of the different disciplines and to do that in such a way that fits you and fulfills your ambition. You should become a specialist in the fields you really like or are inspired by, and on top of that you should become a generalist in fields of further interest. With that attitude during your studies and in the early phases of your career you will find your way into the future that fits you and your ambition best.

JB: *What do you mean by a generalist in fields of further interest? And is there an ideal type of learning environment?*

DG: I mean, they should make sure they don't spend all their time on subjects of inspiration and ambition only, but to also spend time on subjects of interest to

gather a broad perspective. The best type of learning environment is an environment that teaches you the basics of the profession in such a way that space is left for exploration of fascination. In other words: an environment that dictates the minimum basics and that is fully open and flexible for further personal exploration within the field of the profession. In my time at the TUE, I felt the environment was very close to my ideal environment.

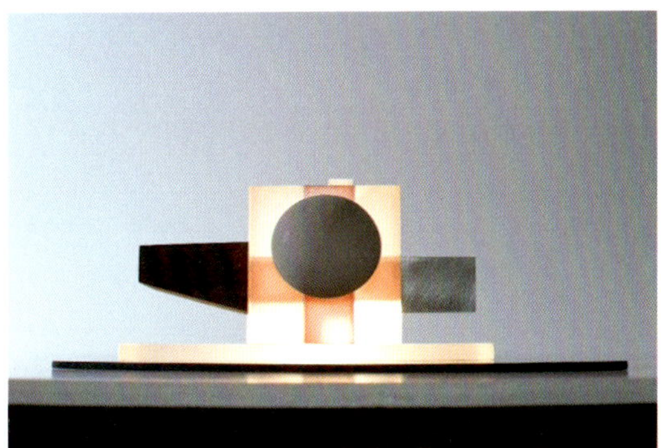

model of taipei performing arts centre in taiwan; david gianotten and rem koolhaas standing in the building as being realized

graduation project: 'green care farm "the sheepfold" by gijs burg, an architectural study on an alternative dwelling for elderly suffering from dementia.

care = the process through which the design of buildings plays a role in translating social agendas for care into a functional built environment while considering a quality of use. each time period has another idea and agenda for a bathroom, a prison, a hospital, the adequately designed environment for taking care of elderly people, etc.

behavior in shape

bernard colenbrander | graduation projects laurence bolhaar and femke stout

The studio Behavior in Shape sheds light on two building species that have fulfilled a prominent role in society through the ages. Hospitals and prisons, emotionally perhaps associated with quite different atmospheres, are here taken together due to their common origins. Relating these buildings to the theme of 'care' implies that both their raison d'être is control and supervision, although with a different motivation. The supervised seclusion of a hospital aims to cure, while that of a prison aims to punish. How such aims work out in building language was taken as the starting point for our studio. Beyond researching how control and supervision are made effective in executed designs – by retracing their origins in history and redrawing their composition – we also investigated the topic from another perspective than that of the building itself, namely the perspective of the inhabitant and visitor. The crucial issue was to imagine how a permanent check of behavior is experienced by the people that are forced to use these buildings.

A helpful concept for such double investigation into these building and their effects is typology, one of the central academic domains of the architectural discipline. To understand the creative and intellectual realm of typology, one has to begin with the smallest component of the system: the type. A type is, in building language, a summary of the most essential features of a certain social function in space. Taken together in a typology, types form a corpus of knowledge that circumscribes a building evolution of millennia, probably with the myth of the primitive hut as a starting point projected into its deepest past.

Just as in nature, selection is a basic medium in the long evolution of architecture. The historical process of architecture is itself a story of invention, a story that describes how changing functional needs have led to a variation in programs that have been converted into buildings by designers, inevitably connected to a fanning out of typological order. It is attractive to assume that such a process will automatically be a stimulus for augmenting diversity, certainly in circumstances of relatively cultural freedom like those we have experienced in our part of the world for centuries. Human actors can be expected to consciously promote diversity when they have the opportunity to explore life on their own accord.

If such has ever been the case, however, modern times - and certainly postmodern times - have shown otherwise. But the earlier phases of architectural development were hopeful. Typological variation was stimulated strongly during the years of early modernity in the nineteenth century, following the enormous expansion of functional needs of the industrial society. In those circumstances it was clear that the Beaux Arts system had to be replaced by more sophisticated genetic sources to produce architecture. The later maxim form follows function did just that, by postulating that buildings had to primarily answer, not to the hierarchy between buildings, but to the specific functional demands of a specific program. It started to be hugely effective in the decades around 1900. While the functionalist creed made in principle each new building a cultural product standing on its own feet, industrial composition and production techniques have promoted a very generic image of buildings designed after World War Two. The building craft, although to a certain level sensitive for the individuality of building programs, became accustomed to the off-the-peg method, resulting in strongly repetitive slab and tower compositions dressed in curtain facades, with geometrical precision "parked in empty space.

This paradox, between specific demands leading to variation in building lay out, and the generic image of architecture in its structure and material presence, is typical for many buildings of the twentieth century. They belong to a voluminous generation of architectural history, but the paradox of being simultaneously individual and generic, was not here to stay. In post modern times the standards of building culture began to shift in the slipstream of more general trends that affected society.
One might say that the paradox, typical for building in the modern period, was turned upside down in the succeeding decades. In essence, while buildings of the post modern era still followed the same standards of industry and possessed structural similarity, the "sameness" of buildings was now being dressed up. A fresh interest in the communicative qualities of buildings caused a dispersal in the architectural vocabularies of decorative effects and motives, historical reminiscences, and the tectonic and colorist tooling of the used materials. But this exuberance of the exterior is not connected with the human actions that occur in the building's interior. Although the repertoire of forms, motives, and surfaces of building craft was extended in those postmodern years, in contrast, building programs began to suffer from the widespread influence of functional genericism. Postmodernism came about in the western world with the reduction of the contents of a building program to a monoculture.

Buildings in the western world accommodate less and less specific actions, besides what people achieve behind computer screens. Manufacturing and craftsmanship – in its traditional meaning – have disappeared to other regions in the global exchange. This process has frustrated the traditional motor behind the production of typological

diversity. It has now come to waiver that apart from being comfortable, sustainable and, perhaps, attractive, there is no specific content for a building to address.
Is there still a future for the type as a relevant supporting stone for architecture? Such question is particularly germane as, in recent times, there has been a remarkable relative success of mixed or hybrid formulas. Hybrids have gained an amazing popularity. An office building nowadays may have the aesthetic qualities of a domestic interior, and if that is the case, such building will be appreciated by the public for its unconventional looks. If there are at all places left for production of goods in the more developed parts of the world, there is a good chance that these buildings behave more like a laboratory than like a factory. Also here the appreciation such a building enjoys depends on the designer's ability to alienate its character from its function. When one encounters a building in the city that presents itself as a relic of industrial labor, it is certainly not anymore what it looks like, but it has recently been transformed by a fashionable architect into a complex for living or working for the urban creative class.

Returning to the specific theme of our studio, such a trend of alienation can also be identified in recently built hospitals. The impression of a hospital nowadays is not connected to the institutes of cure that we used to know, but the visitor will imagine himself in an environment reminiscent of a shopping mall instead. When he penetrates further into the building complex he will imagine himself not in a clinic, but preferably in a rather homely environment, devised to make him feel comfortable. Similarly, disguise is also a theme within the current design of prisons, where it has become common to exchange the traditional expression of walls and bars for invisible means of control and a more or less friendly articulation of the architecture.

The good thing of this development is that it forces architects - and certainly architects at the beginning of their career - to concentrate on the essentials of their profession. How can we approach the genesis of a building that really does for its imagined inhabitants what it must do? How can we understand what is really needed when you enter, find your way through, or even live in a building? Is it possible to forecast the experience that a building will have, after it is erected in concrete, glass and stone? Do we really need disguise as a means for making a building attractive enough, or can we restate the aspect of function in a vital position?

longitudinal section

exemplary project

These were the questions that inspired the projects in
our studio. The first project presented here has been
designed by Laurence Bolhaar, and it is for a prison
building near Rotterdam. Laurence decided not to
take one of the well-known prison prototypes as a
starting point for composition, but chose a literary
idea, that happily produced a stream of associations.
It all began with considering the prison as a machine
that, although its presence in society may be merci-
less, still was able to produce freedom on the inside.
The composition of this machine was primed by a
research that both concerned literary sources and
bodily experiences. The external wall of the building is
certainly drawn with clear references to the aesthetics
of the sublime, brought to life with great imagination.
Compensating the 'terror' of the external appearance,
one may discover space without specific behavioristic
intentions on the inside.

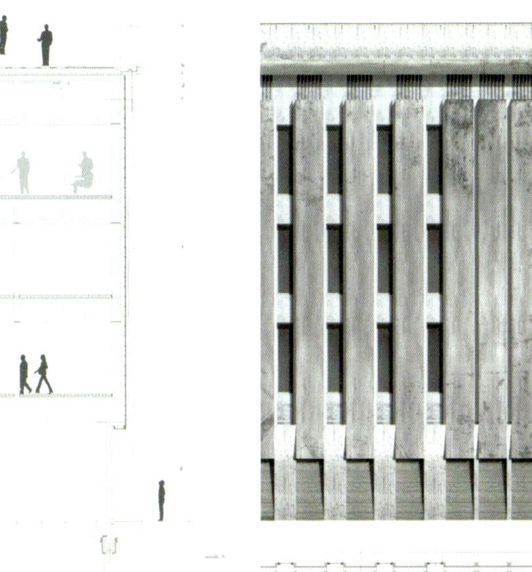

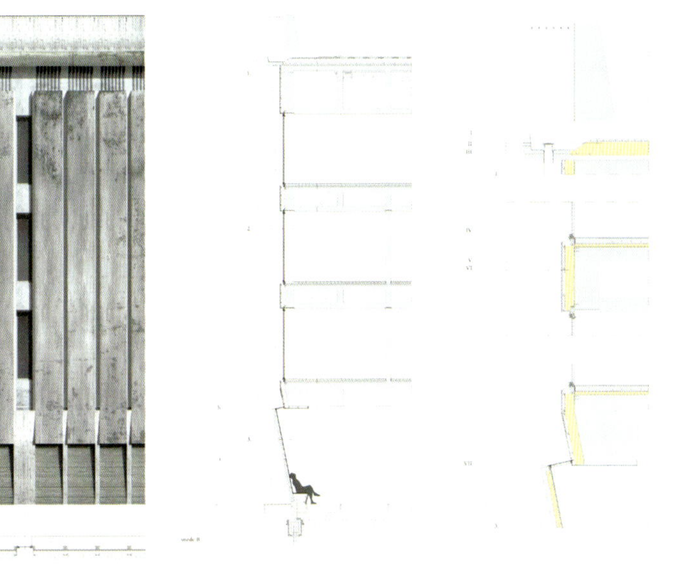

anatomy of the façade

the gallery during the preliminary design, exploring the atmosphere of the space

walking the rhythm of the gallery, guiding you along the four small courtyards in front of the pavilions

the plot (left) is situated in the looiakkes district in the south of eindhoven. the group of houses is connected by a small courtyard to the gallery that encloses a central courtyard. the design needs to provoke the feeling that the heart of the building belongs to the dwellers.

exemplary project

The second design chosen from this studio was designed by Femke Stout and is called *Tout est poésie*. It concerns a mental health clinic, with a location on a plot in Eindhoven. The method she chose to generate her design enjoys also in this case a literary impetus, but is brought into action in a different way than Bolhaar did. *Tout est poésie* is a project that escapes from the tactics of deduction, that are conventional in academic practice. Instead Stout uses a strategy of 'bits and pieces' to collect enough courage to cope with a program for a building in real space and time. Very rare is her ability to emotionalize her design, seeking support in poetry, in particular the unnerving poems of Sylvia Plath.

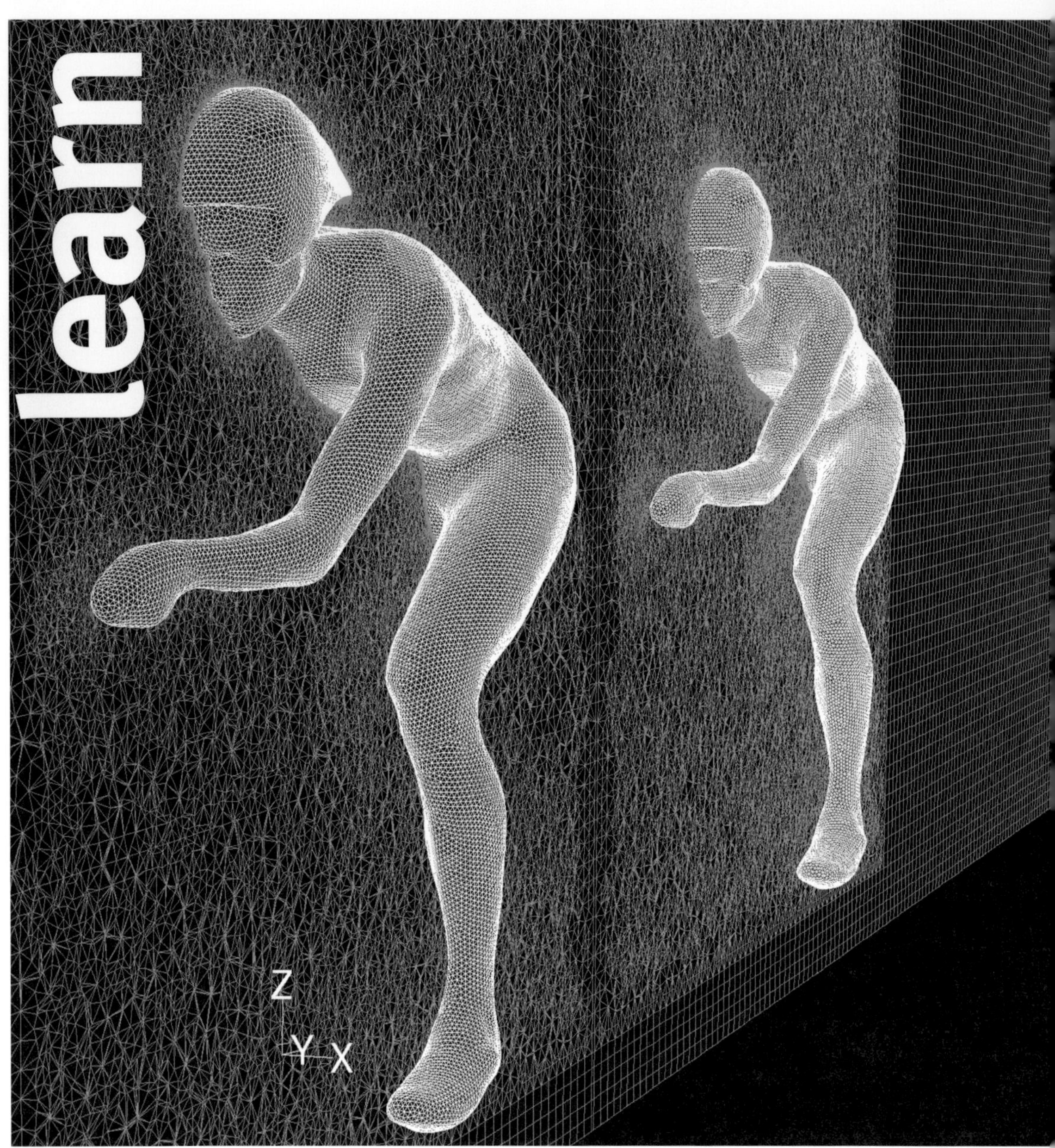

Bert Blocken, Computational Fluid Dynamics grid of two cyclists in time-trial position (Blocken et al. 2012)

learn = improving the technical performance of the materials and equipment of a building

case study bahrain world trade center
wind energy in the built environment

bert blocken | massive open online course

This research report does not question the current Bahrain World Trade Center as a good and functional design. It however concludes that it could have been made substantially better.

The depletion of fossil fuels, the uncertainty about traditional energy supplies, climate change and the growing environmental awareness have strongly increased the interest in renewable energy, including wind, solar and geothermal energy. While most research efforts and practical applications of wind energy have focused on large-scale wind installations in remote off-shore or on-shore areas, much less attention has been given to wind energy installations near buildings.[1-3] The concept of on-site micro wind energy generation is interesting because the energy is then produced close to the location where it is required. Campbell and Stankovic[1] distinguish three categories of possibilities for the integration of wind energy generation systems into urban environments: (1) siting stand-alone wind turbines in urban locations; (2) retrofitting wind turbines onto existing buildings; and (3) full integration of wind turbines together with architectural form. Category 2 and 3 are often referred to as 'building-integrated wind turbines'. Well-known examples of buildings designed with integrated large-scale wind turbines are the Bahrain World Trade Center in Manama,[4] the Strata Tower in London[5] and the Pearl River Tower in Guangzhou, China.[6]

The Bahrain World Trade center was opened in 2008 in Manama, Bahrain. The 150 million dollar project consists of two 240m high towers, with three horizontal-axis wind turbines (HAWT) in the passage between the towers. Each turbine has a diameter of 29m and a rated power of 225kW. The towers and turbines are oriented towards the shore, in order to 'capture the prevailing on-shore Gulf breeze'. The towers are clearly oriented in a so-called 'converging arrangement or V-arrangement', to 'capture' or 'funnel' the wind through the passage.

1. left: reduced-scale model of the bahrain wtc in the wind tunnel. right: computational model of the bahrain wtc for the cfd simulations.

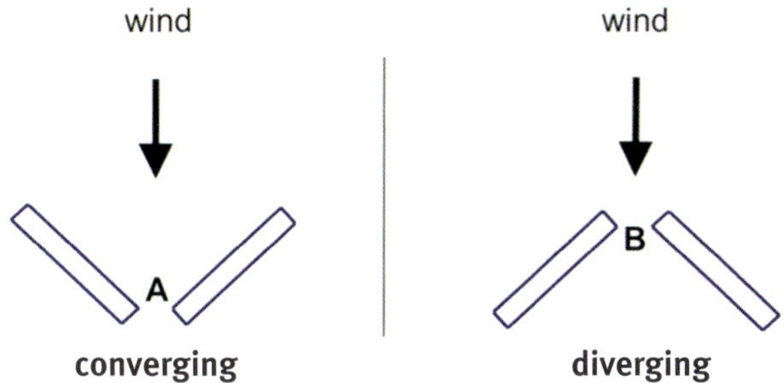

2. top view of two high-rise buildings, left in so-called 'converging' and right in so-called 'diverging' arrangement. the wind direction is as indicated. which case yields the highest wind speed in the passage?

atmospheric boundary layer wind tunnel tests

Our earlier research achievements gave rise to this study, as well as our doubt whether this converging arrangement was the best way to position the two towers. Figure 2 shows a top view of two high-rise buildings, on the left the so-called "converging arrangement" and on the right an alternative; the so-called "diverging arrangement". The wind direction is as indicated. The question is: Which arrangement will yield the highest wind speed in the passage between the buildings (i.e. at point A or B)? We performed this study in 2006 and 2007 by means of dedicated wind-tunnel tests in an Atmospheric Boundary Layer Wind Tunnel (ABLWT) and by numerical simulations with Computational Fluid Dynamics (CFD). The results were published in 2008 in two different scientific journals of the American Society of Civil Engineers (ASCE): the Journal of Aerospace Engineering and the Journal of Engineering Mechanics.[7,8] While intuition might lead one to think that the wind speed will be highest in the converging arrangement, both wind-tunnel tests and CFD simulations consistently showed that the wind speed is highest in the diverging arrangement. The study was performed for different passage widths and for different building heights, but the conclusion was always the same: the wind speed in the diverging arrangement is consistently higher than in the converging arrangement. Figure 3 shows the results from the CFD simulation for buildings with a length of 100 m, a width of 10m and a height of 30m, and for a passage width of 20m (top) and 75m (bottom). The figure displays the amplification factor in a horizontal plane at 2m height. The amplification factor is defined as the ratio of the local wind speed relative to the wind speed that would occur without buildings present. It is therefore a direct indication of the influence of the buildings on the wind speed. Amplification factors larger than 1, imply that the buildings increase the local wind speed, while values smaller than 1 imply that the buildings reduce the local wind speed. Figure 3 clearly shows that the amplification factor is much larger in the passage between the diverging buildings.

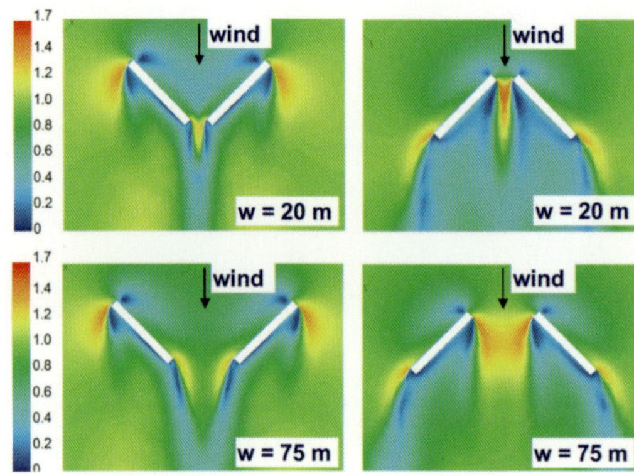

3. top view of wind amplification factor in a horizontal plane at 2m height, for passage width w = 20m (top) and w = 75m (bottom).

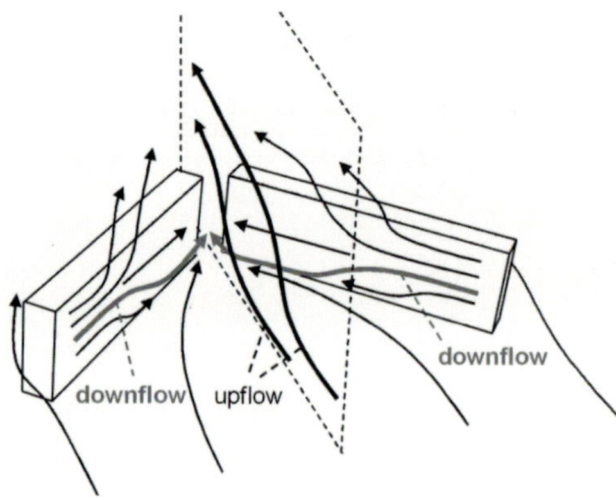

4. schematic representation of wind flow for the converging arrangement. the representation is derived from the results of the cfd simulations. a large part of the wind that approaches the two buildings flows around the outer edges of the buildings, and over the passage. only a small fraction of the approaching wind flows through the passage.

This might seem strange. A frequently heard argument to support the idea that a converging arrangement would yield the highest wind speed, is that the so-called Venturi-effect would occur. This is however not the case. The reason is that Giovanni Battista Venturi studied flows in closed channels, so-called 'confined' flows. When the cross-section of the closed channel decreases, the fluid speed will increase inversely proportional to the change in cross-section. That is the continuity of mass, i.e. the Venturi-effect, as it was defined by Giovanni Battista Venturi himself in 1799.[9] However, a wind flow around buildings is not a confined flow, but an open flow. Not all of the approaching wind will be forced through the passage. Actually, our wind-tunnel measurements and CFD simulations show that most of the approaching wind flows around and over the buildings, rather than being forced through the narrow passage (fig. 4). The reason why the wind speed is higher in the diverging arrangement is simply because the flow resistance in this arrangement is less than in the converging arrangement.

These results led us to question the design of the Bahrain World Trade Center. Therefore, we stated the following research hypothesis: 'The Bahrain WTC would have yielded a higher wind energy output if the buildings were positioned in diverging rather than the present converging arrangement'. In other words: 'From a wind energy point of view, the towers should have been turned 180° around.'

proving the hypothesis

The study was performed with dedicated wind-tunnel tests in an Atmospheric Boundary Layer Wind Tunnel and with numerical simulations using CFD (fig. 1).

Both the wind-tunnel tests and the CFD simulations were performed according to international best practice guidelines to ensure the accuracy and reliability of the results.[10-14] These tests and simulations provided the wind speed at the position of the turbines. Tests were made for different wind directions, for the current "converging arrangement", but also for the "diverging arrangement", in which the towers were turned 180° around. Figure 5 shows the wind speed ratio U/U_{240} in a horizontal plane cutting through the axis of the second wind turbine. U_{240} is the approach-flow wind speed at 240m height. The current converging arrangement is shown on the left side, the diverging arrangement on the right. The position of the turbine is indicated with the black horizontal bar between the towers. It is clear that the wind speed at the position of the turbine is substantially larger for the diverging than for the converging arrangement. However, we want to know the difference in yearly wind energy output between both arrangements. Therefore, the information on wind speed was combined with the statistical data of wind speed and wind direction for Manama, Bahrain and with the power curves of the wind turbines. For the current converging arrangement, our calculations give values for yearly wind energy that are very close to those stated by the designers of the Bahrain WTC: between 340 and 470MWh per year. However, if the buildings would have been placed in diverging arrangement, the yearly wind energy output would have been 14% higher. This is a rather remarkable finding, given the magnitude of this difference and the fact that the integration of wind turbines in the design was the key design feature of the Bahrain WTC.

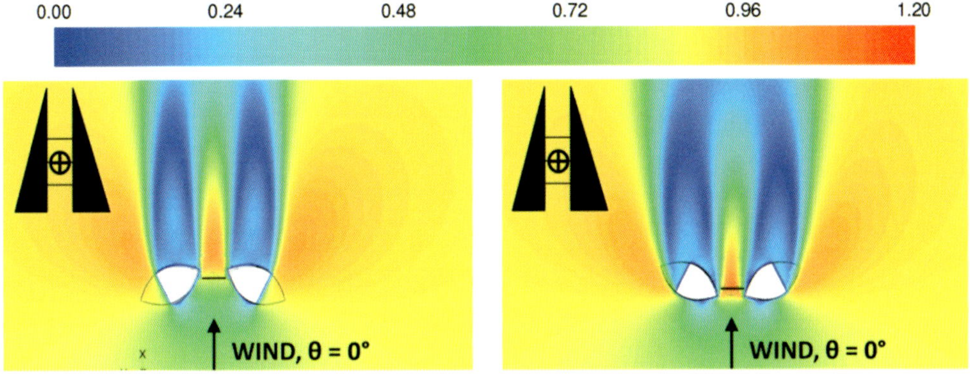

5. top view of wind amplification factor in a horizontal plane at mid-height of the second turbine, for converging (left) and diverging (right) configuration

conclusion

The hypothesis was proven correct. "The Bahrain WTC would have yielded a higher wind energy output if the buildings were positioned in diverging rather than the present converging arrangement".

notes

1. Campbell, N.S. and Stankovic, S. (2001) *Wind energy for the Built environment–Project WEB*, A report for Joule III Contract No JOR3-CT98-01270 2001.

2. Beller, C. (2009) *Urban wind energy – state of the art*. Riso DTU National Laboratory of Sustainable Energy, Riso-R-1668(EN).

3. Sharpe, T. and Proven, G. (2010) Crossflex: concept and early development of a true building integrated wind turbine. *Energ Buildings*, 42 (12), pp. 2365–2375.

4. *Bahrain World Trade Centre* [WWW]. Available from: http://bahrainwtc.com/ [Accessed 08/2011].

5. *Strata Tower* [WWW]. Available from: http://inhabitat.com/first-skyscraper-with-built-in-windturbinesopens-in-london/ [Accessed 08/2011].

6. *Pearl River Tower* [WWW]. Available from: http://smithgill.com/#/work/pearl river tower [Accessed 08/2011].

7. Blocken, B., Stathopoulos, T. and Carmeliet, J. (2008) Wind environmental conditions in passages between two long narrow perpendicular buildings. *Journal of Aerospace Engineering - ASCE*, 21(4), pp. 280-287.

8. Blocken, B., Moonen, P., Stathopoulos, T., and Carmeliet, J. (2008) A numerical study on the existence of the Venturi-effect in passages between perpendicular buildings. *Journal of Engineering Mechanics - ASCE*, 134(12), pp. 1021-1028.

9. Venturi, G. B. (1799) *Experimental enquiries concerning the principle of the lateral communication of motion in fluids: applied to the explanation of various hydraulic phenomena*. Translated from the French by Nicholson W, 1st English ed., J. Taylor, Architectural Library, High-Holborn, London.

10. Franke, J., Hellsten, A., Schlünzen, H. and Carissimo B. (Eds). (2007) *Best practice guideline for the CFD simulation of flows in the urban environment*. COST Office Brussels, ISBN 3-00-018312-4.

11. Tominaga, Y., Mochida, A., Yoshie, R., Kataoka, H., Nozu, T., Yoshikawa M. and Shirasawa T. (2008) AIJ guidelines for practical applications of CFD to pedestrian wind environment around buildings. *Journal of Wind Engineering and Industrial Aerodynamics*, 96(10-11), pp. 1749 1761.

12. Blocken, B. (2014) 50 years of Computational Wind Engineering: Past, present and future. *Journal of Wind Engineering and Industrial Aerodynamics*, 129, pp. 69-102.

13. Blocken, B. and Gualtieri, C. (2012) Ten iterative steps for model development and evaluation applied to Computational Fluid Dynamics for Environmental Fluid Mechanics. *Environmental Modelling & Software*, 33, pp. 1-22.

14. Blocken, B., Stathopoulos, T., Carmeliet, J. and Hensen, J. L. M. (2011) Application of CFD in building performance simulation for the outdoor environment: an overview. *Journal of Building Performance Simulation*, 4(2), pp. 157-184.

building ventilation
basic and applied studies

twan van hooff | staff research

In addition to the aesthetic appearance and structural properties of a building, the indoor environment is another very crucial aspect of building engineering. Occupants of a building should feel comfortable in their working and living environment. Comfort of the occupants depends – among others – on the building acoustics, presence and quality of daylight and artificial light inside the building, the thermal environment to which the occupant is exposed, and the indoor air quality. The latter two strongly depend on the ventilation of the rooms inside a building; i.e. how well the air is being refreshed. Ventilation is used to remove excessive heat, moisture, pollutants, and in extreme cases, fire, smoke and hazardous materials from an enclosure (a room, car, etc.). Therefore, high-performance ventilation of buildings and other enclosures such as airplanes, trains, ships and cars is of primary interest in engineering with respect to human health, (thermal) comfort, energy efficiency, and sustainability.

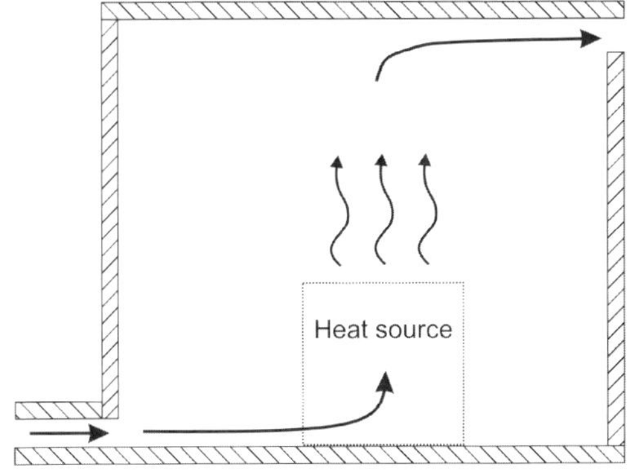
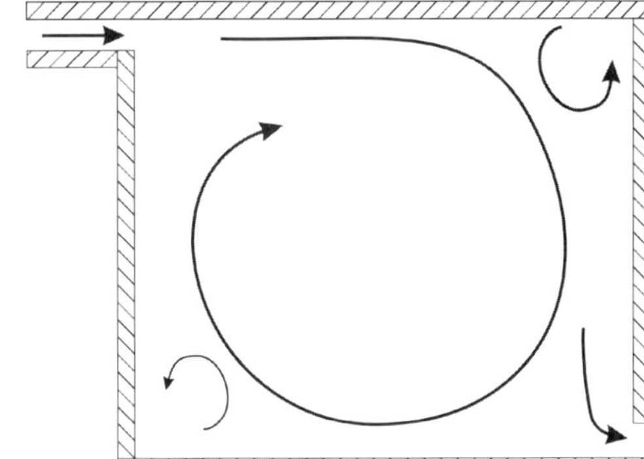

1. schematic representation of room airflow in case of: (a) displacement ventilation; (b) mixing ventilation

The driving forces for ventilation flow can be wind and buoyancy (i.e. natural ventilation), mechanical ventilators (i.e. mechanical ventilation), or a combination of both (e.g. natural ventilation with mechanical exhaust) (Etheridge and Sandberg 1996, Awbi 2003). Irrespective of the driving forces for ventilation, different ventilation methods can be distinguished. The most commonly applied ventilation methods are displacement ventilation and mixing ventilation (see fig. 1) (Etheridge and Sandberg 1996, Awbi 2007). The ventilation method chosen for the ventilation of a specific room depends, among others, on the room configuration, room occupation, designated function of the room, and the possible presence of heat, moisture and pollutant sources. Displacement ventilation is based on the injection of fresh air with relatively low velocities in the lower part of the room. Heat sources inside the enclosure cause a vertically directed airflow and the "old" polluted room air is exhausted in the upper part of the room. This way of ventilating results in a non-uniform distribution of air temperature, pollutants, etc. For this ventilation method internal heat sources are imperative, and therefore it is less suitable for application in residential buildings and other buildings with no of limited heat sources. Mixing ventilation is based on the injection of an air jet in the upper part of the room. The momentum of the jet should ensure mixing of the fresh supply air with the room air, and the diluted air should subsequently be extracted from the room. Attachment of the jet to the ceiling, also known as the 'Coanda effect', is used to ensure that the supply air does not enter the occupant zone too early and helps preventing discomfort for the room occupants (Awbi 2003, 2007). In contrast to displacement ventilation, mixing ventilation does not rely on the presence of internal heat sources to ventilate the room and can therefore also be used in, but is not limited to, (nearly) isothermal cases. Mixing

ventilation can be characterized by relatively uniform distributions of pollutants and temperature.

Since one of the most commonly applied and studied ventilation methods is mixing ventilation, the PhD research presented consisted of two parts which addressed open issues in mixing ventilation research:

1. Mixing ventilation driven by so-called transitional wall jets (low-velocity jets).
2. Mixing ventilation in a large semi-enclosed stadium due to wind and buoyancy.

mixing ventilation driven by low-velocity jets
Since the start of ventilation research in the last century the focus in mixing ventilation research has been primarily on fully turbulent flows, i.e. high-velocity turbulent jets that drive the mixing flow. However, the presence of low-velocity jets becomes increasingly common due to the aim to reduce energy consumption by limiting the airflow rates for ventilation. When one can create a healthy and comfortable indoor environment with a lower ventilation rate, this implies that less air has to be heated or cooled, and less energy is needed for the ventilators (in case of mechanical ventilation). In addition, low-velocity jets are frequently used for ventilating operating theatres, clean rooms, airplane cabins etc. However, up to now almost no studies focused on these low-velocity jets, which indicates the necessity for the study presented here. In mixing ventilation, the jet with fresh – and quite often also relatively cool – air should stay attached to the ceiling long enough for the air to warm up and slow down. If a cold jet enters the zone with occupants too early and with a too high velocity, this can easily lead to comfort (draught) problems. Therefore, the attachment of the jet to the ceiling is very important, but it has not been studied

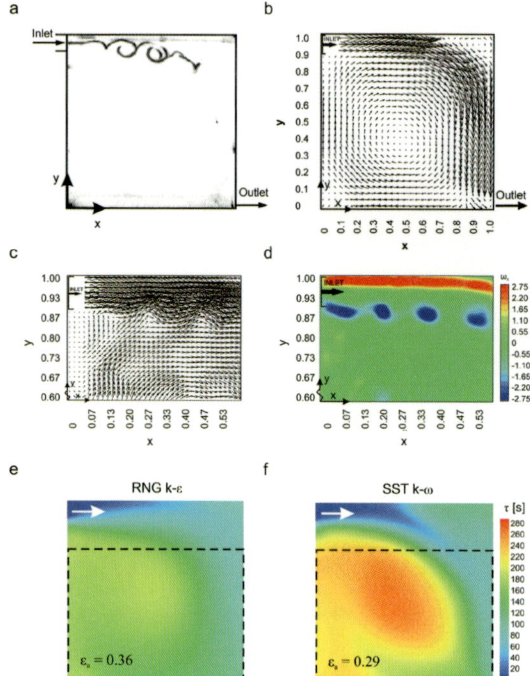

2. experimental (a-d; Re ≈ 1,750) and numerical (e-f; Re ≈ 1000) results of transitional ventilation flow. (a) Instantaneous flow pattern (flow visualization). (b) time-averaged velocity vectors (PIV). (c) Instantaneous velocity vectors (PIV). (d) Contours of vorticity ω_z (PIV). (e-f) Contours of age of air (CFD): (e) RNG k-ε model; (f) SST k-ω model.

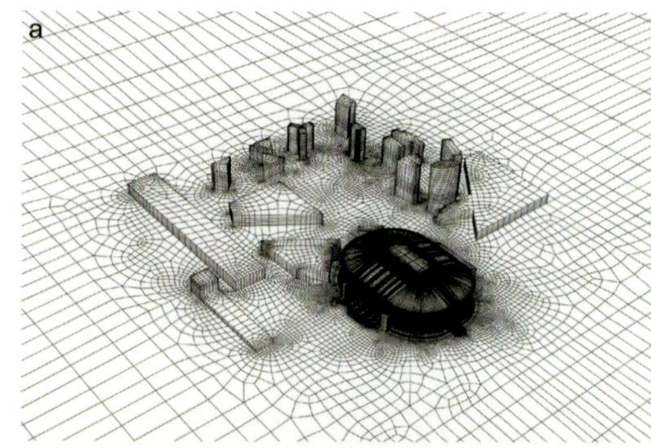
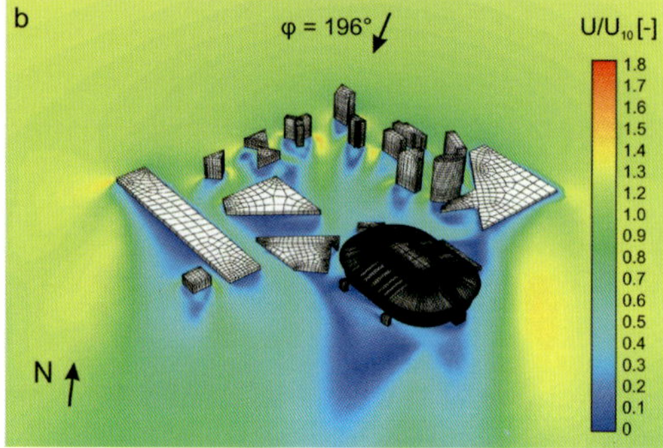

3. cfd simulations of natural ventilation of the amsterdam arena stadium. (a) Computational grid on the surfaces (about 5.5 million cells). (b) Contours of non-dimensional velocity (U/U$_{10}$) in a horizontal plane at h = 8m above the arena deck (U10 = 5m/s, wind direction φ = 196°).

in detail before for low-velocity (transitional) jets. This lack of knowledge can result in comfort problems in ventilated enclosures, and also limits the possibilities to study ways to more efficiently ventilate a room or other enclosure. This study aimed on filling up this void in the international state-of-the-art in ventilation research by performing both reduced-scale experiments and numerical simulations with Computational Fluid Dynamics (CFD) of mixing ventilation flows driven by a low-velocity jet (van Hooff et al. 2012a, 2012b, van Hooff et al. 2013).

The experimental data set that was established includes results of flow visualizations and Particle Image Velocimetry (PIV) measurements of mixing ventilation by transitional wall jets in a reduced-scale water-filled model enclosure (fig. 2, 3). This unique set of experimental data enabled a detailed analysis of the flow in the enclosure in general, and of the flow physics in the wall jet region near the ceiling in particular. Among others, the experiments showed that the separation of the wall jet, and therefore also the flow pattern in the enclosure, are strongly dependent on the velocity of the jet that enters the enclosure. The detachment also occurred earlier (closer to the inlet) than in the case of a turbulent (high velocity) jet.

Furthermore, the low-velocity jet showed the development of discrete vortical structures on both sides of the jet (fig. 2,3), which are typical for these low-velocity (transitional) jets.

The experimental data was subsequently used to assess the performance of numerical simulations with CFD in combination with a range of turbulence models for mixing ventilation flow driven by a low-velocity jet. This comparison showed large deviations between the experiments on the one hand, and CFD simulations with one of the most commonly used turbulence models in the ventilation community on the other hand. This unexpectedly poor result demonstrated the dependence of numerically obtained results of appropriate turbulence models, boundary conditions and other computational settings. The person responsible for the modelling of ventilation flows in practice should have detailed and specific knowledge on the numerical modelling of such flows to avoid large errors.

mixing ventilation driven by wind and buoyancy
Natural ventilation is driven by wind, buoyancy, or most often a combination of both. Therefore, the interaction of the indoor air with the outdoor air plays an important role in the prediction of natural ventila-

tion flow and makes the assessment of natural ventilation more complex than that of mechanical ventilation flows.

The use of numerical simulation with CFD has some clear advantages compared to other approaches. Theoretical and analytical approaches are very valuable to provide general insights but are less suitable when complex geometrical configurations and the associated complex urban wind field are involved. With full-scale (on-site) measurements, many of the influencing parameters (i.e. meteorological conditions) cannot be controlled and the meteorological conditions are intrinsically unsteady (Schatzmann and Leitl 2011, van Hooff and Blocken 2012). Furthermore, information is only obtained at a few sampling positions. In addition, on-site measurements are not an option in the design stage, when the buildings/rooms under study have not yet been constructed. Reduced-scale measurements in a wind tunnel allow controlling the boundary conditions (approach flow, temperatures, etc.), but the measurements are also often only point measurements at a few selected positions. In addition, reduced-scale wind tunnel testing can suffer from similarity requirements that cannot be fulfilled. This is particularly the case for large city models or buildings with small ventilation openings (Reynolds number effects), as well as for non-isothermal wind tunnel experiments (Grashof and Richardson numbers) (van Hooff and Blocken 2012, Blocken et al. 2014).

To analyze the accuracy of CFD for complex natural mixing ventilation flows driven by wind and buoyancy, an experimental and numerical ventilation study was performed for the semi-enclosed Amsterdam ArenA stadium, in its configuration with a closed roof. First of all, full-scale measurements were made that were used to analyze the indoor airflow and the thermal conditions (air temperature, relative humidity, etc.). Furthermore, these measurements were used to validate CFD simulations of the airflow in and around the stadium (= ventilation flow). Subsequently, it was demonstrated that CFD models can be used to successfully assess the current and possible alternative ventilation configurations to see whether the ventilation flow, and thus the indoor air quality and thermal comfort, can be improved. It was shown that improvements of ventilation rate by up to 43% could be achieved by implementing some small geometrical changes in the stadium envelope (van Hooff and Blocken 2010a).

As a last step, the influence of the urban surroundings and the influence of the wind direction on the ventilation were analyzed, showing the effect of the urban surrounding (fig. 3) and thus the importance of incorporating the urban surroundings in natural ventilation studies, and the need to model a range of wind directions to obtain accurate results for the ventilation rates. Excluding the urban surroundings can lead to large overpredictions of the ventilation flow rate (van Hooff and Blocken 2010b).

In summary, it was shown that CFD can be a very powerful tool to predict mixing ventilation flows in naturally ventilated complex buildings. However, the results are strongly dependent on the modelling efforts taken, and validation of the model using full-scale measurements is highly recommended to provide confidence in the results obtained.

conclusion

This study aimed at improving both the basic and applied knowledge of mixing ventilation flows in buildings, which can consequently be used in practice to improve indoor thermal comfort and air quality, and thus to improve the general quality of a building and its perception by the occupants. Mixing ventilation is a topic of ongoing basic and applied research within the Building Physics group of Prof. Blocken at the Department of the Built Environment in collaboration with Prof. Van Heijst of the Department of Applied Physics at TU/e.

references

Awbi, H. B. (2003) *Ventilation of buildings*. London: Spon Press.
Awbi, H. B. (2007) *Ventilation systems: design and performance.* London: Taylor & Francis.
Blocken, B. (2014) 50 years of Computational Wind Engineering: Past, present and future. *Journal of Wind Engineering and Industrial Aerodynamics*, 129, pp. 69-102.
Etheridge, D. W. and Sandberg, M. (1996) *Building Ventilation: Theory and Measurement.* London: Wiley.
Schatzmann, M., Leitl, B. (2011) Issues with validation of urban flow and dispersion CFD models. *Journal of Wind Engineering and Industrial Aerodynamics* 99, pp. 169-186.
Hooff, T. van. and Blocken, B. (2010) Coupled urban wind flow and indoor natural ventilation modelling on a high-resolution grid: A case study for the Amsterdam ArenA stadium. *Environmental Modelling & Software*, 25(1), pp. 51-65.
Hooff, T. van. and Blocken, B. (2010) On the effect of wind direction and urban surroundings on natural ventilation of a large semi-enclosed stadium. *Computers & Fluids*, 39(7).
Hooff, T. van. and Blocken, B. (2012). Full-scale measurements of indoor environmental conditions and natural ventilation in a large semi-enclosed stadium: possibilities and limitations for CFD validation. *Journal of Wind Engineering and Industrial Aerodynamics*, pp. 104-106, 330-341.
Hooff, T. van., Blocken, B., Defraeye, T., Carmeliet, J., and Heijst, G. J. F. van. (2012a) PIV measurements of a plane wall jet in a confined space at transitional slot Reynolds numbers. *Experiments in Fluids*, 53(2), pp. 499-517.
Hooff, T. van., Blocken, B., Defraeye, T., Carmeliet, J., and Heijst, G. J. F. van. (2012b) PIV measurements and analysis of transitional flow in a reduced-scale model: ventilation by a free plane jet with Coanda effect. *Building and Environment*, 56, pp. 301-313.
Hooff, T. van., Blocken, B. and Heijst, G. J. F. van. (2013) On the suitability of steady RANS CFD for forced mixing ventilation at transitional slot Reynolds numbers. *Indoor Air*, 23(3), pp. 236-249.

optimizing the quality of steel fibre reinforced concrete

mark wijffels | graduation project mark wijffels

Previous studies on the failure mode of Steel Fibre Reinforced Concrete (SFRC) slabs made clear that the horizontal fibre distribution sometimes differs with as much as a factor three. This inhomogeneous fibre distribution makes it hard to set up proper regulations for the material and it results in safety factors higher than necessary. Because of the absence of these regulations, the construction industry is reticent in the use of SFRC. When I had the chance to pick a subject for my final thesis, I was glad to be able to continue in the field of SFRC under supervision of Professor Theo Salet.

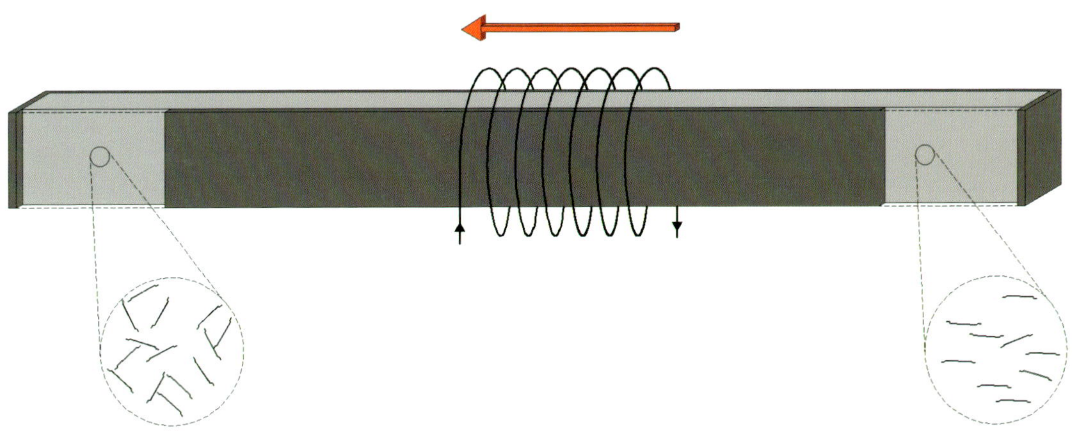

a method to align fibres to the span direction in a scfrc beam. an electromagnetic coil can be shifted over a freshly casted beam. left: fibres unaligned. right: fibres aligned.

In my opinion, the inhomogeneous fibre distribution can be solved by using the present fibres more optimal. Experiments indicate that the optimal fibre angle with respect to the main tensile stress is 10 to 30 degrees Celsius. Bending tests performed on SFRC beams with aligned fibres show a post-cracking behaviour which is significantly improved in comparison with beams that contain completely non-aligned fibres. If it is possible to improve the bending moment capacity of Self-Compacting Fibre Reinforced Concrete (SCFRC) at a constant volume fraction of steel fibres, it is indirectly possible to decrease the volume at a constant bending moment capacity. By increasing the efficiency of the present steel fibres, it might be possible to construct more durable and cost-efficient. If it appears that orienting steel fibres in SFRC improves the mechanical properties of the composite, new research possibilities will open up. Research on replacing stirrups by oriented steel fibres could be conducted. Since stirrups are labour-intensive, a significant cost reduction could be achieved.

Steel fibres are ferromagnetic. That makes it possible to orient them by means of a magnetic field. In this research, a new method to orient fibres has been developed. A magnetic field is generated by running a current through an electromagnetic coil. The fibres in a freshly casted beam will consequently tend to align to the magnetic field lines, which are directed in the span direction of the beam. The coil is shifted over a freshly casted beam in order to orient all metal in the beam correctly. It is important that the field is homogeneous to prevent all the steel from clustering. The method requires a conditioned environment and is therefore suitable for the prefab industry. Self-Compacting Concrete (SCC) is commonly used in the prefab industry and the method therefore focuses on SCFRC. For the practical application of the research, Math Pluis of Spanbeton, active in the prefab industry, acted as a soundboard.

The main purpose of this research was to orient steel fibres in such a way that the bending moment capacity of the composite SCFRC could be improved. The first step in this research was to design an electromagnetic coil in order to be able to generate a magnetic field. To gain the knowledge to design an electromagnetic coil Professor Leo Pel, head of the group Transport in Permeable Media, was contacted. Together we designed a coil to be used on an available power supply and amount of copper wire. The coil has been built with specialist equipment at the university and was used to investigate the behaviour of a single fibre in a magnetic field. Because concrete is not a transparent suspension, an alternative was searched. Silicon oil was chosen because the medium is translucent and has similar rheological properties as SCC.

After experiments showed that it was possible to orient a fibre in the silicon oil, the interaction between multiple fibres was studied. Multiple fibres have the tendency to cluster, causing the formation of chains of fibres. Sven van de Bulck studied this behaviour by performing test on fibres that were attached to each other and single fibres. It appeared that the single fibres are more effective. The chains are thus an unwanted side effect, since the fibres are then not fully embedded in the composite anymore.

Concrete is a suspension of smaller and bigger particles, it would therefore be interesting to see if orienting a fibre still happens in such a material. Tests on silicon oil with included particles were performed. It appeared that the fibre was able to orient, even with the presence of aggregate. Again chains of fibres were formed.

After the research on fibre level, the study was extended to SCC. To be able to predict the behaviour on construction level, the research concentrated on small beams.

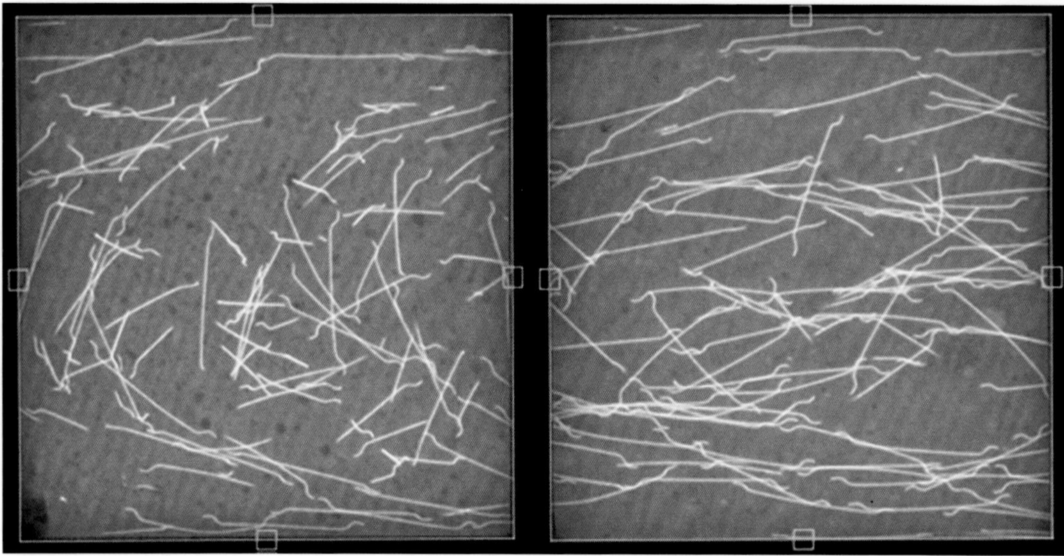

left: unaligned fibres in self-compacting concrete. right: result of aligned fibres in self-compacting concrete

By experimental research, the effect of the governing parameters on the fibre orientation was studied. Because the electromagnetic coil that was used for small scale experiments was too small, a new coil had to be designed. The diameter of this coil is 300 millimetres and has been constructed with the kind help of Opijnen Consultants BV. A wooden rail was constructed to be able to move the beam exactly over the middle of the coil.

One of the most important parameters is the mixture that is used. SCC is different from a normal concrete mixture as it contains superplasticizer which makes it possible to fill moulds without the need of compaction. However, even a small amount has a big influence on the ability of the concrete to flow or to segregate. The perfect mixture for orienting fibres is a mixture that does not segregate but yet remains homogeneous. It should not harden to fast, in order to be able to orient the fibres in the magnetic field in time. To achieve this, a mixture has been designed, based upon a PhD study from Steffen Grunewald at Delft University of Technology. It was modified to achieve a more constant workability for over an hour. The rheological properties were then tested by using a rheometer, with the kind help of Roel Schipper. The concrete was rotated within a container, while simultaneously a measurement was performed on the resistance the concrete showed against the movement. These tests were performed at Delft University of Technology.

After fine-tuning the mixture, test beams were casted to determine the velocity and the magnetic field strength that would be needed for an optimal process. The beams were evaluated by using X-ray imaging. Tineke van Helvert kindly made it possible to use the X-ray equipment at Fontys Paramedic College in Eindhoven. Twelve different combinations of velocity and field strength were tested. The X-ray images were evaluated by using the software ImageJ. The fibre angle with respect to the main axis was then calculated. The combination that gave the best results was used for performing mechanical tests. By making use of a compression bench, the capacity of oriented and non-oriented beams was tested.

It appeared that the increase of the flux density enhanced the alignment of the fibres to the field lines. However, it had negative consequences on the homogeneity of the fibre distribution. X-ray imaging revealed that the fibres had an increasing tendency to cluster. The process of orientation did at first not lead to an increase in bending moment capacity. This does however not mean that the method is useless. Characteristic for the executed test was that the specimen failed at the weakest cross-section. The weakest cross-section was however artificially created by exposing the specimen to a magnetic field which resulted in clustering. The specimen then failed at the point where the least fibres were.

To reveal the full potential Rob Wolfs has carried out additional tests. He compared the behaviour after cracking – the post-cracking behaviour – between beams with aligned fibres and fibres perpendicular to the span direction. He used a testing method that is not prone to fail at the weakest cross-section, but at a predefined point. The test showed a considerable increase in the post-cracking

test set-up to align fibres in self-compacting concrete

electromagnetic coil

behaviour. The assumption that an increase in capacity could be gained is therefore correct. This opens up new investigation possibilities on both method and fibre type. Research should be carried out to minimize the effects of the clustering of fibres. The type of fibre used and the way of casting are promising factors that can improve the bending moment capacity.

conclusion

This research is a result of combining theoretical knowledge of multiple disciplines and has led to an innovative method for improving the efficiency of SCFRC. A challenging experimental program was carried out, which concentrated on the development of a new method, mixture design and visualizing orientation. The prefab industry will have to make an effort to be able to successfully apply the results of this research in practice. The choice is to increase revenues gradually without risk or to apply innovative methods to beat the competition. That requires guts, like it did for me to perform this pioneering research

the transformation of breda's periphery

ad de bont and hans snijders | graduation projects simone camp and merijn de veer

The urban design task in the Netherlands and across great parts of the Western world is to reinforce the existing city. No longer is the agenda the absorption of demographic and economic growth via city expansion, but about improving quality in the existing city. This graduation atelier focused on quality improvement in a mid-sized city. Breda lies strategically in the southwest of the Low Countries. On one side it lies in the shadow of Zuidvleugel, Brainport and Vlaamse Ruit, and on the other it is linked to international axes such as the A16 and the high speed rail line to Germany. Breda has a lot of opportunities and for that reason these projects took into consideration the potentials that come with this strategic position. A differentiation needs to be made: one part of quality improvement concerns post-war housing districts, while another concerns urban areas in transformation such as old industrial parks, abandoned harbor areas, and military barracks. Taken together, these projects offer a complete overview of today's challenges and approaches to benefit mid-sized Dutch and other cities for years to come.

Simone Camp and Merijn de Veer's projects investigate how, given the current context of a retreating, facilitating government, limited investor interest, and a greater demand for initiatives for residents and society, urban restructuring and questions of transformation can be given form. Central to this is the question of what this means for the urban design instrumentarium: what kinds of strategic plans are needed and which lasting development models can be employed? In these projects the role of urban and spatial design are investigated as concerns peripheral zones (Simone Camp - Haagse Beemden Breda) and cultural inheritance (Merijn de Veer- Seeligkazerneterrein Breda). First, using a design study and analysis the social question and the specific conditions of the location were brought into focus. Both plans place a high priority on involving the greatest number of citizens in developing and improving spatial quality, its nourishment, yet ultimately also in the actual construction of the city.

Simone Camp and Merijn de Veer's projects each show how (citizen) participation can lead to interesting forms of urban design. Their projects show that these forms of organic development ask for another type of plan and new forms of control. We consider here Simone Camp's project first in which a new park zone is developed as an intermediary between the landscape and the Haagse Beemden district. We then move to Breda's Old Town where the former military Seeligterrein is to be transformed into a lively corner of the city.

exemplary project

One can justly call the residential district Haagse Beemden revolutionary. Yet this district, built in the 1970s, has slowly reverted to a status quo in which the old opposition of city and countryside reappears. The design for this residential quarter by J.L.M. Tummers and Prof. F.M. Maas was certainly innovative. By 'listening' to the landscape they built an uncommon form: an urban area encircling a green, rural estate zone. Soon after completion it appeared that what had been set aside for agriculture within this cramped landscape was too small resulting in a financial fiasco. Now that the neighborhood is busy with a rejuvenation, it is time to deal thoroughly with the city-land issue. Simone Camp maintains that the internal landscape of the district with its historic rural estates has been cherished as a hidden treasure for too long, as if it were another world which lay outside of urban planning and use. Many views and the positions of buildings as well as functional relations between the city's districts and the countryside have been cut off. Camp links rejuvenation of the district with the landscape question. She introduces a new inner edge to the border between city and countryside. She developed this new edge as a real, peripheral park. It functions as a kind of buffer, a soft intermediate zone between the hard edge of the city and the surrounding areas.

This new soft intermediate zone glues the landscape to the district in a spatial and functional sense. Slices will be made such that the district once again has a view towards the landscape. New hiking and bike paths will be laid such that the district's green middle area will become a strategic link for recreative services. Sports fields will be rearranged such that space is made to link the rural estate zone with the expansive meadows in the north of the city. The new soft intermediate zone fluctuates in depth as needed. It is an architectonic combination of built facilities and natural elements, of historic and new layers. It includes not only a recreative program, but challenges the existing neighborhood to make new edges with a view towards the landscape. Thus the emancipation of the city and countryside will happen place by place and sub-project by sub-project.

City and countryside will embrace one another by means of small projects designed to give form to the new intermediate zone. Each sub-project is part of the whole. The internal, green middle area can be transformed step by step into a large landscape park in which an urban program and a pastoral landscape experience are combined. Camp includes a green investment fund to be run by residents, external financiers and the city. This fund will put those

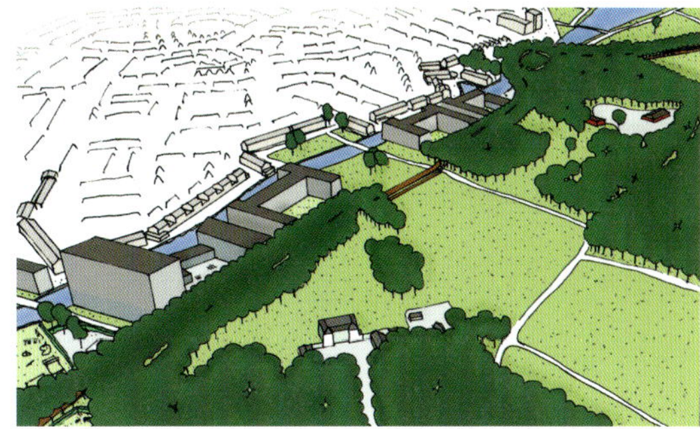

bird's eye view sub-project: urban dwelling

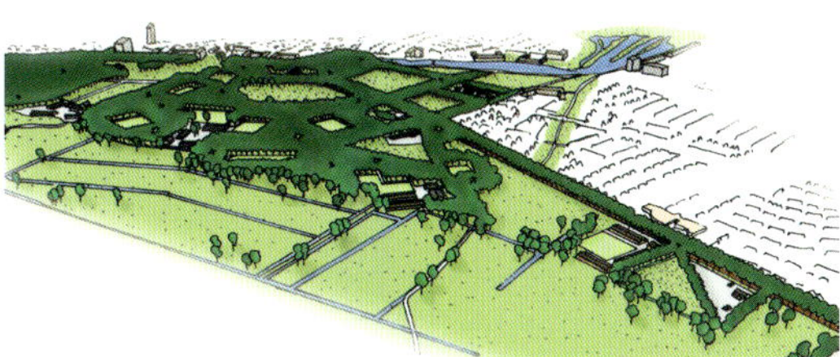

bird's eye view sub-project: sportive oriented dwelling

bird's eye view sub-project: sportive oriented dwelling

bird's eye view sub-project: rural hub

section sub-project: rural hub

section sub-project: sportive oriented dwelling

section sub-project: urban dwelling

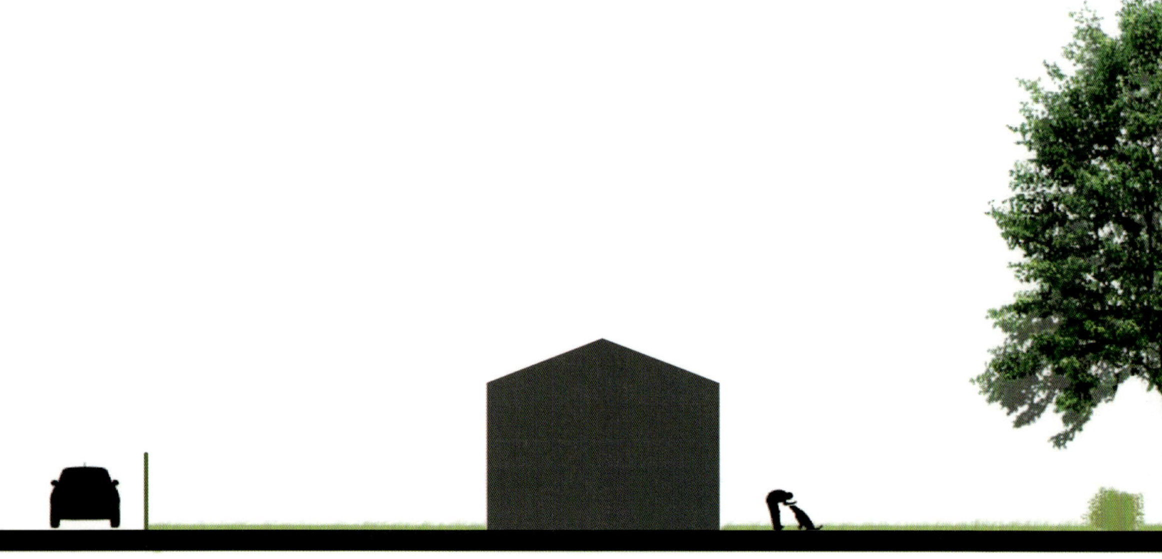

section sub-project: urban playing

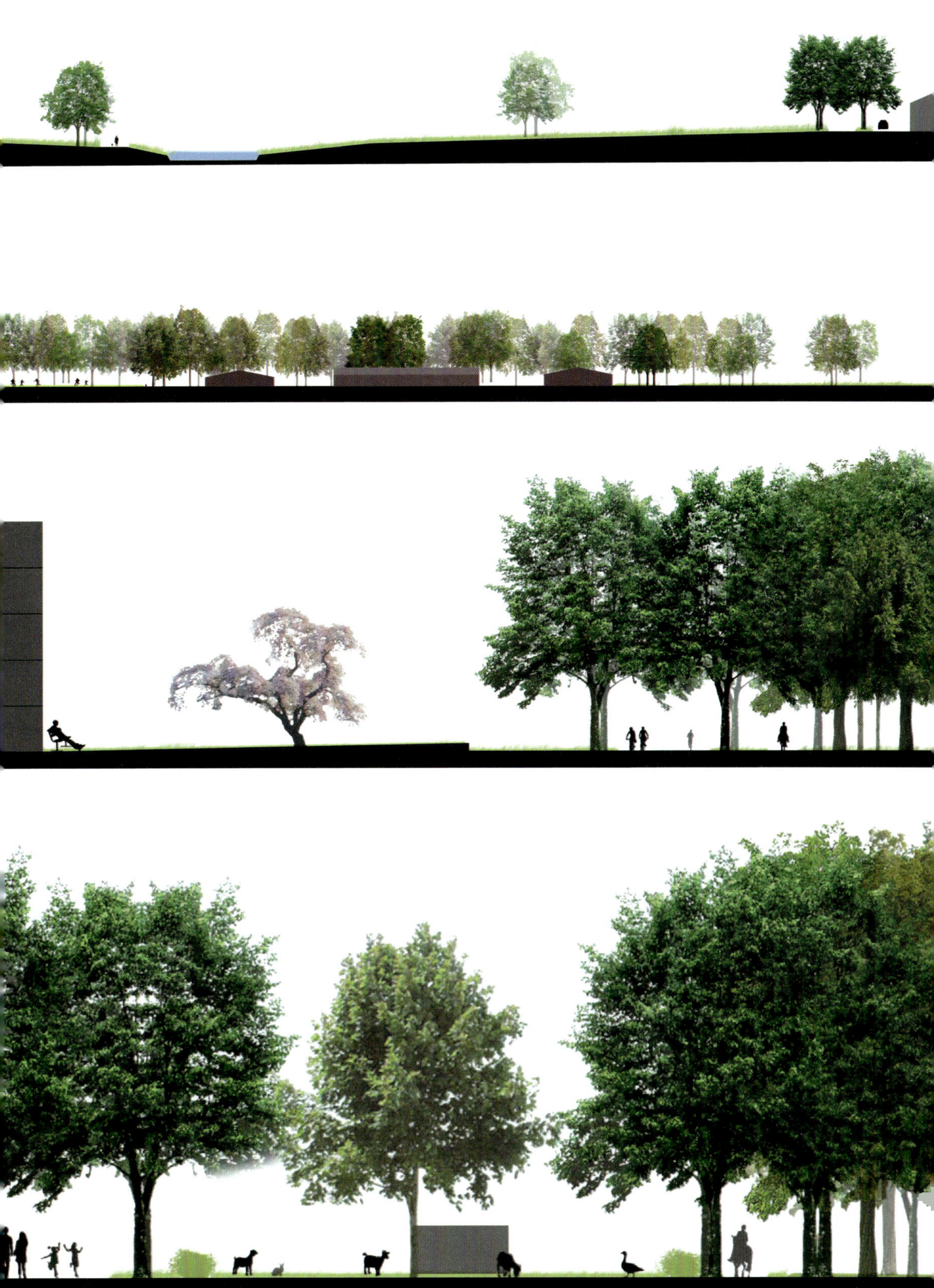

involved in a position to reinvest profits from the area back into quality improvement for the district and management of the landscape. It is even possible to see communal projects funded this way, such as a recreational path through the park or to redevelop the neighborhood in some places and give primacy to the landscape. In the end, Camp puts forward a plan that engages current issues. This is no great landscape or top-down driven design, but a smart, strategic plan in which small spatial-landscape interventions, financed by small development, contribute to the future of a district. Via small interventions a rosy future awaits the Haagse Beemden.

exemplary project

Merijn de Veer's project also addresses a constellation of open and closed spaces, green thinking, and the edge of the city. What is of special interest here is that its inner city location. While in many Dutch and European cities during the nineteenth century urban development took place where city walls had once stood, in Breda this part of the city remained in the hands of the military. Now, a century or more later, the Seeligkazerne has become available as a consequence of the Chassépark (designed by OMA). Merijn de Veer knows that Breda is a city with many parks and that this location is best suited not for a park, but for a residential program. After all, a piece of the city could have arisen here a hundred years ago. The central question is how we can create an ambitious residential program at this juncture. What is clear is that as concerns use, look and strategy this location will be given a function entirely different from that of the Chassépark. Was that project a success? Yes, it put the city on the map with an appealing plan and Breda received international attention. Yet one might ask whether the Chassépark is a piece of the city or primarily a loose collection of buildings? We believe the latter. Public and commercial functions were largely excluded from the project or set on its edges, its relation to ground level is distant, and the residents hardly encounter one another on the street. This lesson makes clear, however, that urban life is not created by buildings, but through (the interaction of) residents.

Merijn de Veer takes this as his point of departure and puts forward a strategy in which residents themselves are able to build homes: a district by and for residents. He is looking for a strategy to create new collective values in the area given very little investment and proposes a three-step process. He suggests that initially the old training grounds be opened to locals. Grant permission for any activity: space for joggers,

barbeque areas, city events, art shows, etc. That is how urban life is generated. People can appropriate a space and the first hiking and park structures can come from this temporary use, to be consolidated later. Other steps should be taken simultaneously. A watercourse, currently missing, can be dug. Those buildings which serve no economic purpose, such as the old tax office and the historic military buildings, can be freed up for diverse urban functions. In this way, step by step, the area can be made useful: an urban guerrilla that slowly takes over the military bulwarks.

This is how, without large initial investment, a popular and accessible urban area can be created. It will be popular because it shirks formal concepts; it will be accessible by virtue of its low investment threshold. It will open the way for unconventional users. It will be a diverse collection which will produce a lively public space. And then...in time initiatives for a self-built residential area can begin. The area's popularity and its proximity to the Old Town make this attractive. The expectation is that residents and financiers will gladly invest in this location in order to build their dream houses.

There is, however, no such thing as citizen participation without rules. Merijn de Veer has set out some rigid rules for the city to develop a new, green district. The initial park structure is to be developed into an interesting sequence of small, green parks. This green network, together with the gardens, will turn it into a special, green low-rise location. Exceptional in this plan are the single-family homes with deep gardens out front. A green park system that facilitates a network of new public spaces is necessary in order permit the city access to the diversity of self-made communities. De Veer's expectation is that, in contrast to the Chassépark, what we will see develop here is a lively and diverse piece of the city. This will be a place that will not come about all at once, but which can grow and adapt. This project shows well how gradual, well-governed development as well as citizen and communal initiatives can lead to an attractive city in which collective urban values are secured.

final design concept

framework of the public space

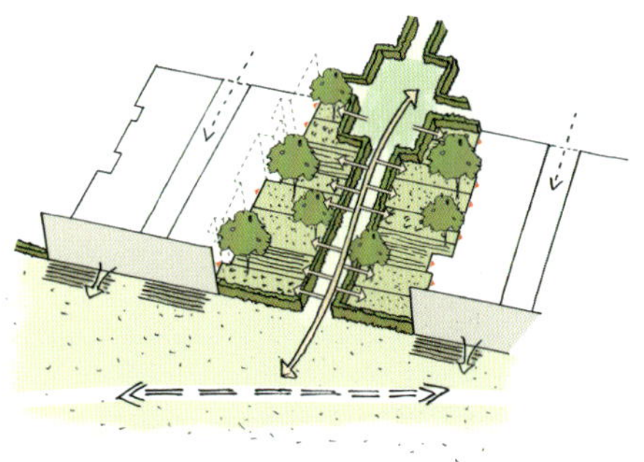

typology of the inverted center area

conclusion

Both of these project investigate the context in which urban transformations might take place, within which time frames changes can occur, who must be involved, which development principles are feasible, and what kind of urban planning can provide adequate control. It is in any case clear that these questions are new and that within the government, the market and among residents there is little knowledge of how to begin to rejuvenate these transformations. It takes time to admit that traditional models no longer work while other models are also capable of producing interesting urban design: a form that is organic, adaptive and which recognizes that cities develop via an interplay of collective and individual initiatives. Urban design is a discipline with a long view, certainly in these difficult times. It is a process of experimentation, repeated testing, and, when necessary, readjustment. In short, we learn by doing.

impression of the center area

hermit house 'jean', 2014, designed by daniël venneman and mark van der net (www.hermithouses.nl)

live = innovating and rethinking existing protocols for living

transportable co2-neutral houses for single-person households

rudy van beurden | graduation project rudy van beurden

What are the requirements for CO2-neutral single-person households on vacant land in the Netherlands?

Increased individualization affects the formation of households in the Netherlands. Young, single home seekers experience difficulties in their search. What is available is often too expensive and existing homes are mainly for families. Additionally, vacant building plots prove unmarketable as investors are reluctant to invest and home seekers tend to rent instead of buying a house nowadays.

Construction company Heijmans seeks to turn their vacant building plots into profitable assets. In an online discrete choice experiment (DCE) a draft design of a portable CO2-neutral house is presented to various respondents. 75% of respondents saw the draft design as 'positive'. They also stated their preferences for a separate bedroom, high energy efficiency and the padded version of the proposed concept.

This research has led to the construction of two prototype homes in the summer of 2014. The aim of the prototypes is for potential residents, decision-makers and investors to embrace this new concept in order to generate new opportunities in the Dutch housing market.

1. design tim van der grinten

Looking at the current number of houses sold, one might ask: 'Are we going downhill?' The number is historically low. Decision-makers are fuzzy about their intended policy for the Dutch housing market. Banks are careful with lending money to both starters in the housing market as well as for the development of real estate projects. Because of the high level of unemployment, many people face problems paying their mortgage or rent. Furthermore, uncertainty and fear about future economic development dominate consumers' feelings: consumer confidence has dropped since July 2011 (Dutch Central Statistics Office, CBS). Rising energy prices have driven up overall housing costs. The trend toward individualization is clearly noticeable in the Netherlands. This results in single-person households with smaller budgets for accommodation, than multi-person households might have.

Single-person households are having difficulties finding suitable accommodation. The overall demand for affordable accommodation for singles is high. The Heijmans firm owns vacant building plots, also known as land positions. The challenge tackled within this graduation project involves bringing these two together.

research purpose
The aim of the graduation project is to bridge the gap between the needs of a growing group of potential customers, single-person households, and Heijmans' vacant land positions. How can these two parties help each other to jointly create a new reality that is profitable for both? The aim of this research is to provide information for a business plan that links the demand of the home seeking singles with a feasible business offer that is promising for the company. This research must make visible the preferences of potential residents, regarding a proposed draft design of a single-person home.

The scope of this research is limited to the elements needed to present a feasible business plan upon which a company can base an investment decision. Furthermore, a scientific methodology will be used to research residents' choices. The research will be limited to the Netherlands as this is the housing market with which all stakeholders are familiar.

A literature study has been performed to underpin the research undertaken in this graduation thesis. Roughly three fields of interest where investigated: the Dutch housing market, energy efficiency for buildings, and the psychology behind individualization, identification and changing values.

the dutch housing market
The current housing market shows a decrease of new houses. Renting, rather than buying, has become more popular among starters. It is expected that half a million single-person households will be added to the total number of households within the next twelve years (to 2025). The current housing stock, which mainly consists of single-family houses, will not meet the needs of all these new households. As current market conditions do not promise short-term improvement, it remains difficult to develop permanent buildings on vacant land positions. Yet there may be feasible temporary solutions. Buildings could be temporarily placed on vacant land for a maximum stay of five years, based on a temporary building permit.

Both residents and policy makers have gained improved awareness about the need for building energy efficient, as our built environment accounts for a large share of all CO_2-emmisions. Residents prefer technical improvements to their homes, rather than having to change their behaviour or consumer patterns. These findings make it worthwhile to emphasize the development of CO_2-neutral houses.

2. design tim van der grinten

As consumers identify themselves with products or services that touch their personal values, it is essential to consider the impact of values within any type of industry. When designing a specific accommodation it is worthwhile to take into consideration the values of single-person households (based on Rokeach, 1979). These can include the need to feel free and to live a comfortable life (terminal values) as well as having self-control and being independent (instrumental values).

developing a transportable co2-neutral house
A new, integrated housing concept is not easily developed individually. Knowledge from various experts is needed in order to present a realistic proposition. Help was sought from various professionals for this project. This intense collaboration eventually resulted in a realistic draft design of a compact, transportable and CO2-neutral house. The design consists of two modules each made of timber. Both modules are transported to the final location where one is placed on top of the other.

As affordability and energy efficiency are vital ingredients for the housing market nowadays, these aspects have been elaborated within the housing concept from the very start. The houses can be equipped with photovoltaic panels and solar water heaters that provide electricity and hot water in an environmental friendly and cost effective way. At the conclusion of this graduation thesis it was still unclear which installations were to be implemented in the design.

To be able to predict which housing design will be most welcomed by potential residents their decision-making behaviour had to be researched. In this project a 'Discrete choice experiment' has n been used. This research technique is distinct from other conjoint methods because preferences are elicited by asking respondents to choose one alternative from those presented, rather than asking respondents to rank alternatives, or give them a rating. The goal of discrete choice experiments is to understand and model the behavioural process that leads to the respondents' choices. Within this graduation thesis this tool is been used to research respondents' preferences regarding the proposed housing solution.

The information provided and the questions were kept to a minimum to keep the survey as appealing as possible. The first screen asked respondents to participate in the survey. Given only some basic information about the displayed attributes and two images of the draft design of the house, people were asked to fill out eight unique choice charts. Figure 3 shows an example of one of these choice charts.

households for single households

set of choices - choose the alternative of your preferene:

features	alternative I	alternative II	neither
maximum rental period	max. 5 years	max.3 years	
energy	average (labeled A)	average (labeled B)	
finishing upholstered	upholstered		
total costs monthly	550 euro	650 euro	
housing type	1 room apartment	1 room apartment	
collective space	without	without	

your choice: ● ● ●

3. sample choice chart with explanation of the attributes

conclusion

Almost 75% of the residents perceived the proposed housing design as 'positive'. Respondents participating in the survey especially preferred the alternative that covered the maximum rental period of five years. An excellent energy label (A+++ label) had a great positive contribution to a given set of choices. A separate bedroom (2 room apartment) is also highly preferred above a studio. Preferably, houses are padded and not furnished. Also, no communal space is required, as respondents do not appreciate these extra offerings.

In short the conclusions can be wrapped as follows:
- There is a huge market for single-person accommodations: 500,000 extra single-person households will emerge in the upcoming decade (to 2025, CBS '13). About 71,000 of these will be from people 25 to 34 years of age;
- In order to present a healthy business case, the maximum cost (excluding VAT) per house should be 60,000 all-in (transport, profit, etc.);
- The maximum renting period (5 years), having a separate bedroom and an excellent energy performance (label A+++) are very important to potential renters. It is worthwhile to invest in an energy generating system beforehand as the result can lower monthly costs;
- Respondents do not require communal space or a furnished accommodation.

münchen, *rekonstruiert*

haike apelt | graduation projects mark gijsbers and erik van de scheur

The graduation ateliers of the Rational Architecture chair, led by Professor Christian Rapp, are devoted to the morphological and typological analysis of the European city. The ateliers focus on a specific subject related either to a specific (morphologic) feature or to a broader contemporary urban problem. All ateliers share an interest in the critical relationship between the idea and form of the city and the architectural project. The tradition of rationalism in architecture and the notion of type provide the theoretical background of this interest.

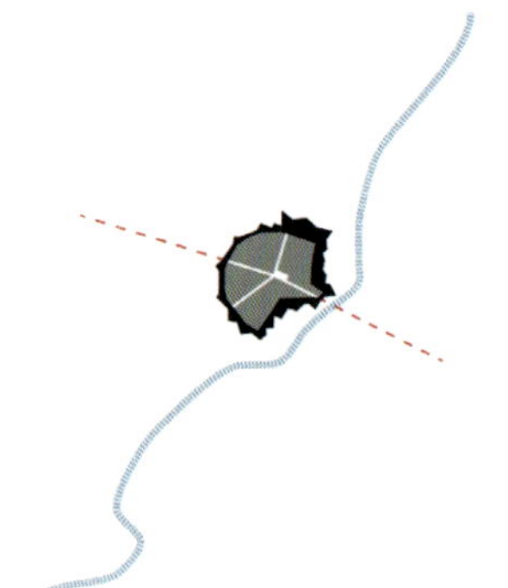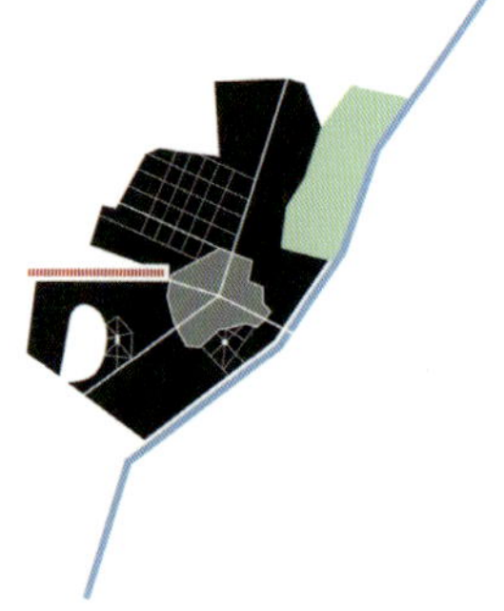

critical phases in the development of the city

The ateliers start with a typo-morphological analysis of the city and the exploration of a general theme. This is a collective effort, carried out in the first semester, which results in a so-called 'atlas', consisting of a sizeable number of analytical drawings and texts. In the analysis we study the morphological development of the city, its genesis and transformation in relation to the underlying socio-cultural, political and economical mechanisms in order to understand the different spatial and typological phenomena. The analytic work forms the basis for the definition of individual design subjects in the second semester. Here the aim is to make the actual project instrumental by answering an individually proposed research question. Thus we see the drawing not simply as a tool to (re)present a thought or concept, but as a tool to actually gain knowledge about a specific spatial problem and ultimately about architecture in general.

The graduation atelier *München, rekonstruiert* continues this design-based research method. Concentrating on the critical relationship between architecture and the city, the urban analysis carried out in the first semester stretches across time and space. Munich, which was heavily destroyed in the Second World War (almost 90%) poses a special case as concerns the question of urban reconstruction. Unlike cities such as Berlin or Dresden, which took their destruction as a chance to construct a new city according to new ideals, Munich chose to rebuild with only slight alterations, an approach known as the "Münchner Weg". The urban plan of the inner city was accurately re-drawn, the streets re-stored, important facades re-constructed. Where possible, the historical example was to be followed, otherwise it was advised that it should "nach modernen Gesichtspunkten, aber im Sinne der Altstadt neu und frei gestaltet werden, damit wir in einigen Jahrzehnten unser liebes München wieder

index 1933 - 1958

white   built footprint 1933
red   built footprint 1958

haben wie es war." [be designed from a modern perspective, but in accordance with the Old City new and free, so that in a few decades we once again have our beloved Munich as it once was] (Karl Meitinger, 1946) Munich's identity was to be restored by the reconstruction of the city's historical image.

Today the city (still) faces a great shortage of housing and is (due to the favorable economic climate) expected to grow continuously in the next decades. The large-scale housing production of the last years, dominated by private investors, has resulted in rather nondescript developments that lack the urban qualities and vitality of the inner city or even of earlier (pre-war) examples of collective housing. In order to open a debate about how to deal with a further increase in population urbanistically and architectonically, the German periodical *Stadtbauwelt* dedicated issue 26/2012 to the question "Muss München dichter werden?"

[Must Munich become more densely settled?]. The answer, whenever inner city qualities are concerned, is obviously yes. We took this hypothesis as a starting point and tried to find specific places in the city which carry the potential for densification in a way that challenges existing urban models. While some students chose to study public building types, related to the city's research and education activities, the majority of the students focused on the problem of housing. With the typo-morphological research as a starting point, the German term *Weiterbauen* [to continue building] served as a concept of 'building-further' on existing urban forms and types, while taking into account changed sociocultural conditions and in effect changing the existing types. *Weiterbauen* therefore is part of a general discussion about the European city as well as a very specific discussion about the possibilities of urban densification and revaluation in Munich today.

cross section

exemplary project

Erik van de Scheur's research focuses on urban villas in Munich, a form which constitutes one of the foremost building commissions of the nineteenth century, especially in Germany. Mostly built in ensembles, called 'villa-colonies', this type of housing still characterizes many quarters at the edge of Munich's city center.

While the roots of this building type can be traced back to the *villa romana*, the middle-class villa became tremendously popular in the sixteenth century, with the Venetian villas of Andrea Palladio as a main reference. For the wealthy middle-class the representative country estate served as an escape from busy city life. It was a place of contemplation supplying the joy of 'simple' country life. The search for physical and spiritual beauty was reflected in the architecture with its sound proportions, painted interiors and views into the surrounding countryside. Positioned on higher terrain, the villa was also to demonstrate the social position of the family. These principles Erik still finds to be apparent in the middle-class villa that appeared at the end of the nineteenth century. The so-called *Gründerzeit* [founding period], characterized by rapid industrial expansion in Germany, was when the new middle-class acquired wealth and influence while that of the monarchy and nobility was declining. This new status involved a more expensive lifestyle and fitting accommodations, a demand which the freestanding, representative villa at the edge of the city was able to answer. In the development of the suburban villa, which became the affordable type for a broad middle-class, Erik finds two ideas to be influential: the importance of the family (the interior) and the relation with the landscape. Yet the suburban villa, he writes, "was a compromise between life in the country and life in the city. The ideals of the country villa, with its representative appearance, its revaluation of family life, a private domain of peace and quiet, and its strong relation to the landscape, were merged with those of the townhouse. It generated a new typology that grew to be the most important building task of the *Gründerzeit*: the suburban villa, or *Stadtvilla*."

The concept of the ideal villa (representation, views to landscape, interior) form the point of departure for Erik's villa design in the *Wiesenviertel*, the oldest of Munich's villa colonies. The theoretical research of the villa-typology provides the architectonic vocabulary, a thorough analysis of the historical development of the *Wiesenviertel*, and the urban and architectonical rules, the specific form of the design.

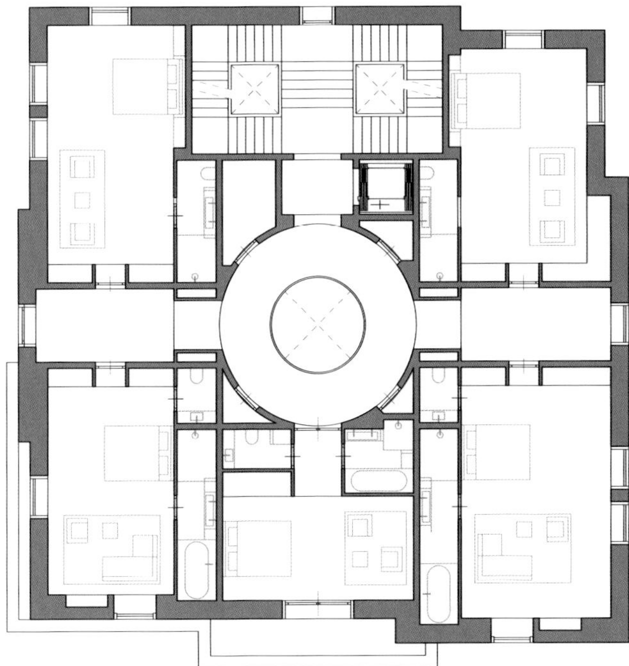

floor plan first and second floor

The quarter is characterized by monumental urban villas orientated towards the *Theresienwiese,* where the annual Oktoberfest is held. In recent decades several alterations were made that appear to threaten the coherence of this ensemble. Erik's aim is therefore "to develop a modern interpretation of the 19th-century 'Wiesenviertelvilla' via a typo-morphological analysis of this historical context so as to ensure the preservation, continuation and enrichment of the characteristic cityscape of the *Wiesenviertel* and *Bavariaring.*"

"Research revealed three overarching themes which typify the urban villas of the *Wiesenviertel*: spatial hierarchy, ordering elements and its relationship with the (urban) landscape. [...] These three themes have subsequently formed the basis for the design of a compact and luxurious hotel on the *Bavariaring* which both typologically and morphologically has its origins in the 19th-century urban villas. Typologically, the themes emerge in the concatenation of representative rooms on the *piano nobile*, which are linked by means of enfilades. In the heart of the building is the round *Diele* which connects the primary functions both horizontally and vertically with each other.

On the first and second floor are the hotel rooms in which tranquility, intimacy and the relationship with the landscape are essential. The upper two floors also focus on the landscape and feature a stunning panoramic view of the *Theresienwiese* and the Alps. Morphologically, the themes emerge in the sculptural form of the exterior. This form is a direct derivative of nearby urban villas, making the volume instantly recognizable as a typical *Wiesenviertelvilla.*"

The resulting slightly odd, yet distinctive external form of the villa, which clearly calls upon the specific context of the *Wiesenviertel,* is being combined with a carefully composed interior that brings the richness of the typological research to a conclusion.

references
(Karl Meitinger: Das *Neue München, Vorschläge zum Wiederaufbau.* München, 1946)

impression of the urban villa within its historical context as seen from the theresienwiese

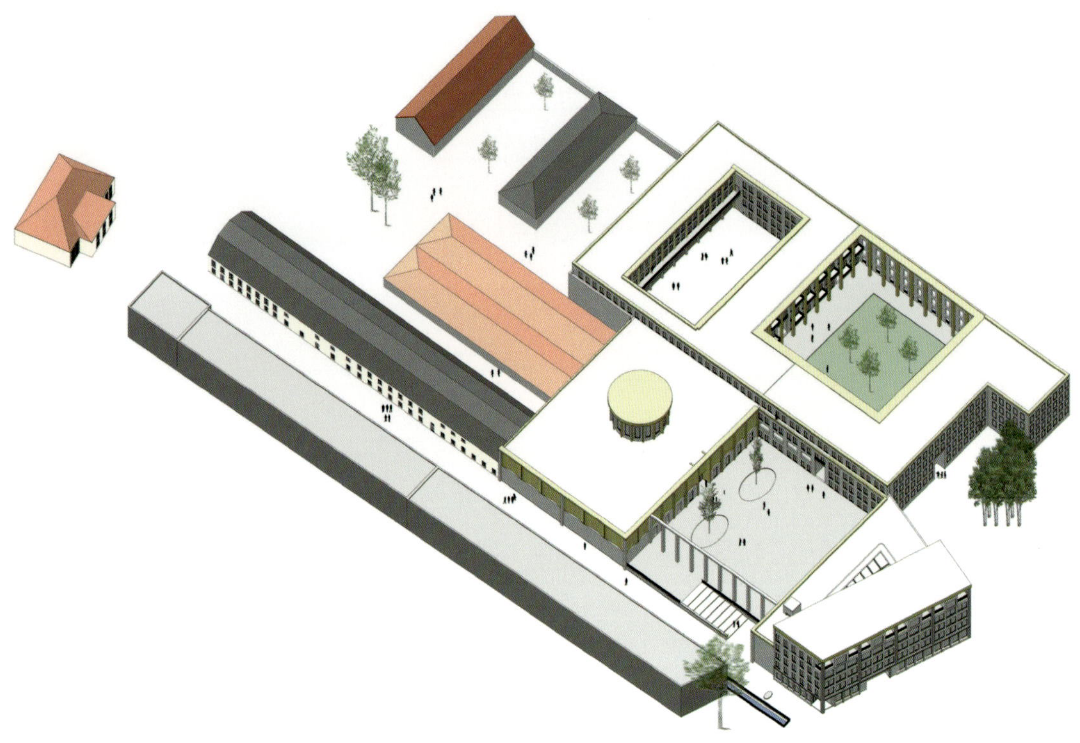

exemplary project

Mark Gijsbers' project starts from the fascination for morphological phenomena and an interest in architectural theories of the 1960s and 70s. Two foremost sources inform his research: Aldo Rossi's *L'Architettura della Citta* (1966) and Colin Rowe & Fred Koetter's *Collage City* (1978). Rossi's reading of the morphology of the European city is based on the distinction of Primary Elements ('monuments' of the city) and the texture of the surrounding urban fabric, made up of dwellings. Together they form the 'urban artifact' (*fatto urbano*) which includes the built environment as well as the city's history and daily life. This distinction proved helpful in the typo-morphological analysis in understanding the morphological structure of Munich. Mark observes that while "drawing the ground plan of the Nymphenburg-Neuhausen quarter in Munich, Nymphenburg Palace seemed to act as a Primary Element", which he defines as "a building(complex) characterized by a long-term presence in the city, a structuring effect on the urban tissue [and] a catalytic effect on the urbanization." Analysis further reveals a possible reading of the urban structure as a collage, in which 'composites' (a term borrowed from C. Rowe) could act as infill between different urban patterns. His definition reads as follows: "Composite architecture is characterized by a double legibility as an architectural object and urban texture. They also play a role in urban spatial sequences and/or create interior worlds." As hybrids between Primary Elements and the urban tissue, Composites form the focus of Mark's research. In order to fully understand their characteristics and behavior examples are analyzed. Analysis reveals the great richness and complexity of form the Composites can take in order to answer very different urban demands which leads to the following conclusion:

"The Composite is not a typology, but it can be classified according to shared characteristics:
1. creates spatial sequences, either urban of internally;
2. makes use of objects in the mass of the building in order to strengthen spatial sequence or to order sequence;
3. the building mass is subordinate to the geometry of the enclosed space."

The challenge of the architectural project lies in testing the usefulness of the Composite on a location

dwelling domain

where different, even contradictory, urban patterns
meet. Behind the Schlossrondell the ordering effect
of the Primary Element of Nymphenburg Palace is
no longer perceptible; this produces a 'blind spot'
in the urban fabric. In this disorderly urban tissue
lies an old porcelain factory and a canal that runs as
a hardly recognizable axis all the way to the Olym-
pic Park. The unbuilt area borders different urban
conditions including buildings of different typology,
geometry and scale, and a 'gap' in the sequence of
buildings along the Menzingerstrasse. To strengthen
the visibility of the axis of the canal, which connects
the location to a wider urban scale, its geometry
becomes the 'starting line' from which the design is
constructed. The canal is made visible by a corridor.
Perpendicular to the corridor lie a sequence of urban
spaces consisting of four inner courtyards. The inner
courtyards evidence analogies to spatial proportions
found on the site. The building mass shapes the
spatial sequence while inviting a double readability
as a composition of different objects grown together.
The program, involving a museum for the porcelain
factory, a hotel at the Menzingerstrasse and homes, is
positioned according to the different public character

of each space. The museum is being conceived as
a Primary Element in order to introduce a spatial
hierarchy and serve as an ordering element within
Composite.

The project proposes a working method deeply concerned with the lessons from the history and theory
of architecture on one hand and the reality of the city
(*fatto urbano*) on the other. The atelier succeeded in
making these lessons instrumental and this design-
based research project is thus a valuable contribution
to the experiments of *Weiterbauen*.

jewish traces in amsterdam

jochem groenland and hüsnü yegenoglu

The Anne Frank House is the best known hiding location in Amsterdam.
About many other shelters in Amsterdam from the same period little or
nothing was known, before this research was carried out.
The interdependence of social and spatial reality is one of the core issues in
the research of the unit Architectural and Urban Design and Engineering.
By means of mapping, reconstructing and speculating we try to shed light
on history in its progress, which sometimes is accompanied with drama.
The Jewish case is an explicit example of this priority in our program.

hiding place at the
tweede boerhaavenstraat 77

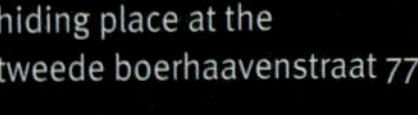

Amsterdam had a thriving Jewish cultural life before it was disrupted in the period of occupation (1940 - 1945). That life has left its mark in the architecture of Amsterdam as can be seen in the buildings of Jewish institutions, theaters, museums, churches, schools, cinemas, cafes and residential complexes. A number of these buildings survived the war and the postwar urban renewal projects, others were demolished and disappeared for ever. The buildings that still stand form the last physical evidence of a forever obliterated urban culture. The traces of the buildings that disappeared are being preserved in archives and memories, its pictures left on drawings and photographs and by these means form a part of the architectural memory of the city.

Before the Second World War the about 80,000 inhabitants of Jewish descent formed the largest Jewish community in the Netherlands. It is noteworthy that, compared to all other countries and cities with a Jewish population in Amsterdam the highest number of Jews was arrested and deported. The reason lies in the efficient registration and classification of citizens established by the Amsterdam municipality of which the occupants made use. In 1940 the occupants ordered the Amsterdam administration to draw the so-called 'Stippenkaart' (points map). This demonstrates that the making of maps is not always neutral and can clearly become a part of a political strategy.

Despite the highly efficient bureaucracy a number of Jews still managed to go into hiding in the city and found shelter in attics, caves and hidden rooms of residential buildings, 'achterhuizen' (back yard houses) and workplaces. Here are shown two examples.

Hiding place in Mansion Willet Holthuysen (1678), in use as Museum Willet – Holthuysen, Herengracht 605 (analyzed by Rob Goetheer, Mariëtte van de Water, Marissa van de Water and Jeroen de Winter). This large urban villa was originally built for the Dutch diplomat Jacob Hop (1654-1725). In 1861, the young couple Abraham Willet and Sandrina Louisa Geertruyda Holthuysen bought the house and moved in. Both were well known for their bohemian lifestyle, surrounded by artists and writers. The couple renewed the exterior and the interior of the house in Louis XIV style, highly fashionable at the time. When the last Holthuysen passed away in 1895, the building was turned into a museum, and has been ever since. During the occupation of Amsterdam, the building was used as a secret meeting place by the Dutch resistance, and also as a temporary hiding place for Jews. Doctor Jo van der Hall was among those who went into hiding here.

Hiding place Tweede Boerhaavenstraat 77 (1911, analyzed by Paolo Apostolides, Natasha Giraud, Thibaut Berges and Jeroen Pelzer). To escape from the mass deportations to concentration camps which the Germans conducted from 1942 on, a large group of Amsterdam's Jewish citizens went into hiding. Among them were Peter Baer who was seven years old at the time, and his parents Felix and Catharina Baehr. They found their hiding place in the Tweede Boerhaavenstraat in the eastern part of Amsterdam. The dwelling was constructed in 1911 and consisted of four floors with a total of sixteen apartments. During daytime the Baehr family lived on the ground floor where they had two small rooms and a toilet. In case of danger or emergency the family hid in a tight basement space underneath the floor.

hiding place at the herengracht 605

proffessor nicolai vasiliev and his wife at the opening of the pykete dome

make = innovating and rethinking existing protocols for making

ice dome

arno pronk | graduation project jorrit hijl and roel pluijmen

The focus of this atelier is on flexible formwork and its environmental benefits. It is related to my PhD research about flexible formwork for fluid architecture and finds its international scientific platform at the IASS (International association for Shell and Space structures) and the ISOFF (International Society of Flexible Formwork)[1].

The challenge is to explore and to develop theory, technology, tools, products and building designs based on flexible forming technology with the materials glass, concrete, ice and composites. Besides the architectural impact, flexible forming can have an environmental impact since it results in a reduced use of resources. The environmental benefits of flexible moulding are in the structural optimization of (lightweight) structures and production techniques with less waste material and less transport. Theoretical research is related to experimental research and the realization of a design, if possible in cooperation with companies or other research institutes.

The growing interest in free-formed structures in contemporary architecture conflicts with the traditional casting processes. The desire to combine the physical and structural qualities of formwork and material with the esthetical qualities of free-formed architecture sparks researchers to strive for new methods to make architecture.

Flexible formwork is in harmony with the rising interest in fluid architecture and the renewed interest in shell structures. The master thesis focusses on the technical and architectural application of curved shell structures in a building design. Technical aspects are: Fiber reinforcement and the treatment of material.

1. In 2015 we will organize the IASS and ISOFF symposium at the muziekgebouw in Amsterdam in cooperation with the TU Delft. I am chairman of ISOFF and project leader of the ice dome projects in Finland that have to be realized within the coming two years.

shell structures by bb con

shell structures by heinz isler

barbapapa by arno pronk et al

shell structure by massimiliano fuksas

pinbed moulding by roel schippers, peter eigenraam

samples of fibre-reinforced ice (pykrete)

In this master thesis by Jorrit Hijl and Roel Pluijmen, supported by other students, companies and volunteers performed the calculation and construction of a 30 meter-span ice dome on an inflatable mould that had to be realized in the winter of 2014 in Finland. This ice structure was the world's largest igloo and the first building realized with fibre-reinforced ice (pykrete). The construction method of the Pykrete Dome consists of a combination of the construction method of T. Kokawa and the relatively unknown construction material pykrete. The construction method has been analysed and adjusted to the Pykrete Dome design. An oversized membrane is inflated under a geodesic rope cover. The inflatable structure is used as a mould for the Pykrete Dome. Water, Snow and pykrete is sprayed in thin layers onto the membrane with a temperature of -8°C or lower.

The construction material pykrete is fiber reinforced ice which can be 3 times as strong as regular ice. The pykrete is applied on the lower section of the Pykrete Dome, where the stress in the shell structure is higher. By conducting various experiments, the construction method has been analysed and improved. High quality sawdust is mixed with water and sprayed onto the membrane with a centrifugal pump and an adjustable nozzle.

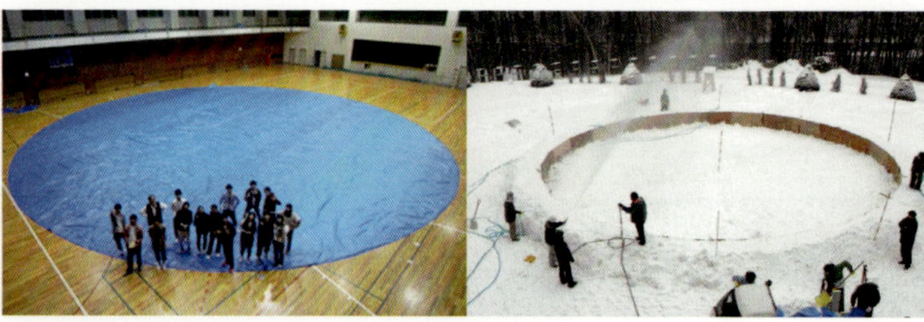
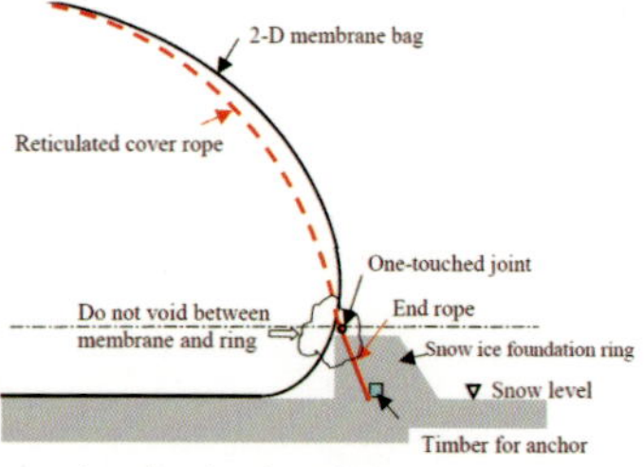

membrane   foundation ring   section drawing foundation

1 Master Thesis Ice Dome

Since 1985 Tsutomu Kokawa has been building various ice dome structures in collaboration with the Tokai University. Until last year, the largest ice dome realized had a span of 25 meter. The information available from the previous realized ice domes and experimental studies by T. Kokawa have been highly interesting in this attempt to build an ice dome with a span of 30 meters. Different studies have concluded that the addition of (natural) fibres to ice structures results in higher strength properties of the ice. For more information about the material properties and the development of shot pykrete, please read the IASS 2014 paper by Pronk, Vasiliev, Janssen and Houben as this research focused on the application of pykrete in the construction and calculation of a 30 meter span ice dome.

The spherical dome was calculated with a surface thickness of 300 mm, a span of 30,000 mm and a radius of 16,800 mm. The dome was calculated by hand and with a numerical model. The model was drawn in Rhino; the numerical calculations were done in Diana TNO. The analytical calculations and the numerical results were compared with each other by which numerical model was validated. Even under extreme circumstances like heavy snow and asymmetrical wind load, the structural behaviour of the shell turned out to be within the limits of the material properties. The maximum calculated stresses were -1.08 N/mm^2 and +1,02 N/mm^2. The laboratory test with 10.5% sawdust in ice proved maximum absorbable stresses of -12.45N/mm^2 and +3.74N/mm^2.

Structural experiments show that the quality of the ice was very high. However, the application of pykrete was lower due to the layered construction in the samples. The compression test with pykrete samples [42% Pykrete, 58% Ice] resulted in a 5,02 N/mm^2 compression strength. These values are 21% higher than regular ice. However, the full strength of pykrete still has to be determined.

2 pykrete

The positive effects of reinforced ice have been known for many years. The inhabitants of northern regions traditionally used lichen to strengthen their igloos [N.K. Vasiliev et. Al, 2003]. However, the first scientific studies in the application of ice composites were in the Second World War by Geoffrey Pyke and his team. After several experiments Geoffrey Pyke learned that a mixture of ice and wood fibres created a strong solid mass, much stronger than pure ice. In our research we experienced that 10% sawdust appeared to provide the best values for both mechanical and processing behavior. This optimized behavior concerns the homogeneousness, the processability, the toughness and strength of the pykrete. The particles of the sawdust have to be small (up to a maximum of 2mm). The compressive strength of pykrete with 10% sawdust can be 12.45 N/mm^2 and the flexural strength can be 3.74 N/mm^2. Compared to regular ice (respectively 3.18 N/mm^2 and 1.24 N/mm^2), the pykrete is three times better. The ductility of pykrete is even twenty times better. With the improved toughness, the pykrete also allows a larger deformation of the structure and reduces crack formations. Pykrete also improves the resistance against thermo shock that might occur during the building process as a result of the spraying of water on the frozen shell structure.

3 spraying of pykrete

The spraying of water was separated from the adjustment of snow on the inflatable mould like in the construction method of Kokawa. In this case the difference with the method of Kokawa is that sawdust was added to the water. A slush of water with sawdust was sprayed into thin layers of snow on the surface of the inflatable mould.

4 kokawa ice domes

Japanese Professor Tsutomu Kokawa has studied the effects and behavior of ice shell structures for many years. In 1985 he started his first experiment with the construction of a 5m and 10m ice shell. These rela-

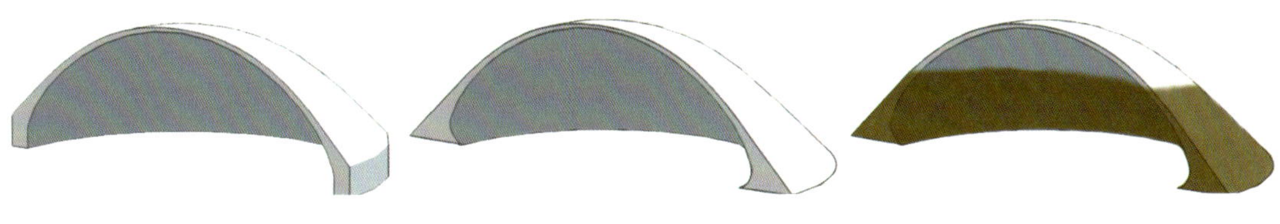

foundation ring of ice foundation with ground anchors with pykrete 'ring'

tively small shell structures gave a good impression on the behavior of the construction material ice and the unique construction method. In 2001 he finished the largest ice shell structure so far: The final dimensions were 25m for the internal span and a height of 9,2m. The construction method developed by Kokawa exists of three important parts: The foundation ring, the membrane with rope net and the spraying of snow and water.

5 pykrete dome.

The final Pykrete Dome design is a result of a combination of various studies. The research on ice shells by T. Kokawa provides a simple and efficient construction method. The construction method is analysed and improved for an optimal design of the Pykrete Dome. The relatively weak and brittle construction material ice is reinforced and replaced with a stronger ductile material Pykrete. By using an almost similar construction material, the construction process can mostly remain the same and is only adjusted where necessary. The Pykrete dome was made by a team of fifty people from the Netherlands, two from Belgium and supported by the local community of Juuka in Finland. The construction time on site was limited to only three weeks. Juuka Finland is one of the coldest regions in the European Union with temperatures of -15°C to -30°C with an average temperature of -11°C in January. Although these statistics, there can be big fluctuations in the temperature. The winter of 2014 was the warmest in 150 years and our building time with a temperature below -8°C was reduced to seven days. To speed up the process and to be more independent of the climate conditions, the foundation system of Kokawa was replaced by the use of ground anchors. First the inflatable mould and the rope cover were placed and fixed to the anchoring points. Next, after inflating the mould, loose snow and ice was applied at the foundation. This process was repeated until a solid, thick snowice foundation ring was created. Due to the possibility to use heavy equipment to construct the foundation ring, the construction time of the

foundation ring was greatly reduced. The foundation required a certain height, width and slope to realize the actual shell structure. To minimize the curvature of the inflatable mould from the ground to the net structure, the inflatable mould had a 10% oversize. In this way the oversized inflatable mould filled the corner between the ground and the rope net and also the bulges between the net and the ribs in the icebecame bigger. The anchors were placed in the ground which can be done at any temperature, but in contrast to the method of Kokawa the anchors cannot be reused at another location. The change in foundation made the dome lower at the same span. For environmental reasons we worked with a PE foil for this is easier to recycle than PVC.

The shape of the Pykrete Dome is Spherical. The internal dimensions have been measured with a laser device. In addition, the location of the pykrete layers have been analysed and documented. Value [mm]

- Span: 29060
- Height [Dome]: 9750mm
- Height [Entrance]: 3100mm
- Height [Pykrete]: 5680 - 6650mm
- Shell Thickness: 150 - 400mm

The thickness of the shell has been measured on different locations in the structure. By drilling holes in the shell, the thickness could be defined. The section shows the graduation in the shell structure from the base of approximately two meter to the top of the shell with only 150mm.

a. inflatable mould

c. spraying of water on mould

b. spraying of pykrete

d. spraying of water with support of firebrigade

vacuumatics: 3d formwork systems

Investigations of the structural and morphological nature of vacuumatic structures so as to be used as semi-rigid formwork systems for producing 'free forms' and customised surface textures in concrete for architectural applications.

frank huijben | doctoral dissertation

One of the architectural trends of the last two decades is commonly referred to as 'digital architecture', which comprises digitally-generated geometrically complex, often irregular, yet fluent double-curved shapes in architecture. Particularly with respect to concrete forms in architecture, a new architectural vocabulary seems to have been introduced altogether. Although advanced digital manufacturing systems are emerging in architecture, the construction processes in general require some sort of boost to 'keep up' with the already heavily advanced (digital) design and analysis processes. For a successful realisation of the desired 'free forms', the focus must lie on the construction process of the (components of the) building structures in close relation to the design and (structural) engineering processes. Although curable materials (such as concrete) are considered particularly useful for the realisation of the desired 'free forms', the formability and the adaptability of the formwork system of choice are considered the limiting factors. The increased interest in 'freely-curved' concrete structures has already led to a wide range of either practically, academically or artistically-derived construction techniques, which are to be divided into three essentially different (formwork) categories, referred to as rigid formwork, semi-rigid formwork and flexible formwork. Semi-rigid formwork systems in particular are considered very effective for the realisation of 'free forms' in concrete.

vacuumatic structures typically consist of an (unbound) aggregate core, which is enclosed by a flexible membrane envelope. these structures obtain their structural stiffness by introducing an internal underpressure (or partial vacuum).

Vacuumatic structures (or simply 'vacuumatics') are identified as structural systems that are composed of an (unbound) aggregate core, which is enclosed by a flexible membrane envelope and structurally stabilised by means of an internal underpressure. The resulting externally acting ambient (air) pressure is causing the membrane envelope to be tightly wrapped around the unbound particles of the aggregate core, hence 'freezing' their current configuration. The state-of-the-art of vacuumatic structures indicates a wide variety of applications in various fields of use, such as: packaging, manufacturing, medicine, architecture, interior design, toy industry and robotics. In the field of architecture and robotics in particular many developments have emerged in the last decade. The semi-rigid nature of vacuumatic structures implies that these structures are very much suitable to be used as a semi-rigid formwork system to create 'free forms' in concrete.

Although the basic structural principle of vacuumatic structures is relatively simple, no analytical definition is known (to the author) that explains the vacuumatic prestressing of the unbound particles of the aggregate core, nor the composite behaviour of the aggregate core and the membrane envelope when subjected to bending loads. In this thesis, an analytical definition is given for the vacuumatic prestressing forces that are to be defined for each individual particle that is in direct contact with the membrane envelope. The resulting internal (contact) forces are examined by representing the vacuumatic structure as a compact assembly of solid discs (in 2D) and drawing a grid from the centre points of the connecting particles (which represents the directions of the individual contact forces).

Some empirical research on the flexural behaviour of vacuumatic structures has indicated that the structural capacity of these structures in terms of strength and stiffness largely depends on the properties of the aggregate core. Little attention, however, is generally given to the contribution of the (tensile properties of the) membrane envelope to the overall flexural behaviour of vacuumatic structures. This thesis explains the systematic and fundamental experimental research that has been carried out for determining the influence of the individual characteristics of the aggregate core as well as the membrane envelope on the flexural strength and stiffness. It needs to be stated, that the total bending strength of vacuumatic structures turns out to be rather limited in general, which typically goes hand in hand with relatively large deflections. Nevertheless, for the best structural performance (in terms of strength and stiffness) a vacuumatic structure ideally consists of a lightweight aggregate with a high mutual friction and a high compressive stiffness. Apart from that, a non-penetrable membrane envelope with a high tensile stiffness is desired as well as a relatively high level of vacuum pressure. The flexural strength and stiffness of vacuumatic structures is greatly enhanced when the particles of the aggregate core are able to interlock. Further enhancement of the flexural strength and stiffness of vacuumatic structures is obtained by adding a sheet of fabric as reinforcement in between the aggregate core and the membrane envelope. This reinforcement ideally has a relatively high breaking strength and a relatively high tensile stiffness.

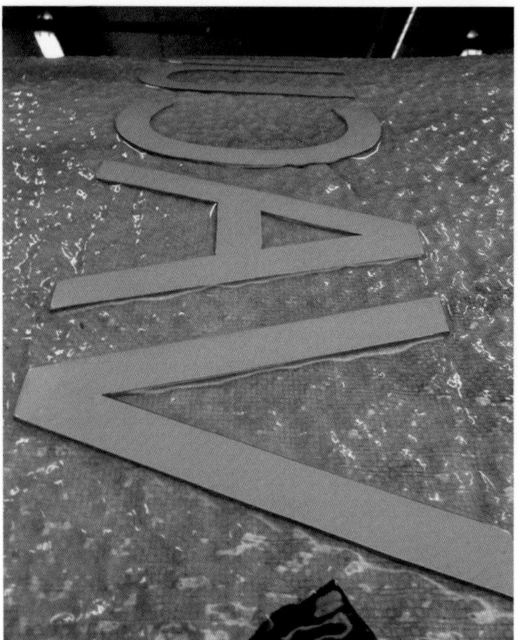

by adding solid objects inside the membrane envelope, a customised surface texture of the intended concrete object can be obtained.

the customised surface texture of the concrete object after removing the (re-usable) vacuumatic structure (or rather mould).

Due to the complex mutual interactions of the (unbound) particles and the flexible membrane envelope, the flexural behaviour of vacuumatic structures can hardly be determined analytically. Apart from that, the internal force distribution throughout the bending process is not measurable from physical laboratory experiments. Therefore, the flexural behaviour as well as the corresponding failure mechanisms of vacuumatic structures are analysed in close detail by means of numerical simulations using Discrete Element Method (DEM) software. The vacuumatic structures are modelled as assemblies of unbound particles (or solid discs in 2D), which are enclosed by a continuous flexible boundary. This flexible boundary is modelled as a closed chain of smaller particles (or 'beads') that incorporates the physical properties of the membrane envelope. This method is referred to as the 'Bead-Chain Method' (BCM). The vacuumatic pre-stressing is simulated by applying an externally acting (vacuum) pressure onto the bead-chain, which effectively stabilises the assembly of unbound particles.

The morphological potential of vacuumatic structures is considered one of the most valuable aspects of this structural system. Based on the analysis of various historical and contemporary applications of vacuumatic structures in different fields of use, it is illustrated that vacuumatic structures are particularly used for

creating sculptural forms (or 'free forms'). The functional shape of vacuumatic structures can be obtained by means of a wide variety of techniques. Four essentially different shaping processes are distinguished, which are referred to as form-defining, form-fitting, form-directing and form-finding. An intriguing aspect of the various applications of vacuumatic structures is that most of them are specifically designed to be (repeatedly) 'freely' shaped. The vacuumatic prestressing of the aggregate core plays a crucial part in defining the formability and adaptability of vacuumatic structures. Without any induced vacuum pressure (0% vacuum), the unbound particles possess hardly any consistency, which enables them to more or less flow freely inside the flexible membrane envelope. A slight increase in the level of vacuum pressure, causes the particles to be slightly jammed, which on its turn results in the relatively easy deformability (or rather mouldability) of the structure. In this semi-flexible state, the assembly of particles is able to be 'freely' shaped, while retaining its newly given shape. In full vacuumatic state (at approximately 100% vacuum), the particles are maximally jammed, which rigidifies the structural assembly and enables it to carry (external) loads. The ability to stabilise or 'liquidise' the particle configuration by simply adjusting the level of vacuum pressure is considered one of the key factors in the shaping process of vacuumatic structures.

a vacuumatic (inner) mould can easily be repeatedly shaped from a rigid (outer) mould.

Various empirical formwork experiments illustrate the potential of using vacuumatic structures as a semi-rigid, adaptable formwork for producing 'free forms' in concrete. The effectiveness of the shaping method of choice is considered of crucial importance. One of the (practical) aspects to deal with when shaping vacuumatic structures by means of a formative shaping process is how to determine the initial configuration of the unbound particles inside the flexible envelope. Based on various shaping case studies, it is found to be beneficial to initiate the (formative) shaping process from a flat surface. Apart from that, the semi-rigid nature of vacuumatic structures makes it beneficial to derive their final functional shape from external (or internal) objects by using a specific form-fitting technique.

Apart from load-bearing formwork applications, vacuumatic structures can be effectively applied in addition to a (rigid) formwork system to produced customised surface textures in concrete. This enables a relatively low-tech realisation of a wide variety of textures by means of one single, re-usable and highly adaptable vacuumatic formwork. In addition, the use of vacuumatic structures introduces a complete 'new' array of shapes in concrete (such as sharp folds and creases), which are typically rather difficult (and thus costly) to produce. Large potential is found in combining the use of vacuumatic formwork with the 'latest' developments in concrete technology, such as Ultra High Performance Concrete (UHPC), Fibre-Reinforced Concrete (FRC) and Self-Compacting Concrete (SCC).

As a 'side effect' of utilising vacuumatic structures as semi-rigid, adaptable formwork systems, a new technique has been introduced for applying concrete mortar. With this technique, a highly viscous concrete mixture is infused through the pores of the aggregate core by inducing an internal underpressure. As a result, the vacuumatic structure is impregnated with a concrete mixture to create 'Vacuum-Infused Concrete' (VIC).

prototype of a kinetic tensegrity structure

arno pronk, harry buskes, lucas klerk and peter koelewijn | graduation project lucas klerk and peter koelewijn

This research presents a design solution for the integration of dual axis sun trackers to lightweight roof structures. This is done with a kinetic tensegrity structure with a stable membrane roof and hinging vertical struts. The struts punch through the roof at the high points of the membrane roof. On top of the struts PV cells are connected that can follow the path of the sun as a result of the kinetic hinging of the struts in the tensegrity.

The orientation of the solar cells is an important factor in its energy efficiency. The best sun tracker therefore would be one that either constantly measures the position of the sun and changes the angles of the solar cells accordingly, so that they are always perpendicular towards the sun. Tracking systems allow solar cells to follow the path of the sun. There are single-axis trackers and dual-axis trackers. With tracked solar cells it is possible to have the same output with less solar cells. This means less weight, less construction and a smaller inverter. A misalignment of 10 degrees will reduce the output by only 2%. A bigger misalignment, however, reduces the output significantly. A dual-axe tracked array of solar cells can achieve an extra energy output of 40-50% compared to a fixed roof array that is tilted ideally for the latitude.

By varying the length of de strings or rods tensegrity structures can be made kinetic, like the movable mast created by Frei Otto in 1976. The goal of this research is to make a light-weight roof structure with a sun tracker by means of a kinetic tensegrity.

Kinetic adaptation can be used to create a sun-tracking roof surface based on the Geiger dome typology. By using a combination of flexible and rigid components it is possible to transform the overall shape of the dome, so that a considerable surface of the roof can follow the path of the sun. In 2013 we proved this with digital and physical models based on the change of length of the cables of a Geiger dome (2013 IASS conference paper by Pronk et al). This movement was achieved by a sliding or hinging of the bars. The solar cells were integrated in a membrane that could slide over the sliding structure of the Geiger dome. In this structure the angle of the cells could change between 27 and 65 degrees. Although the achievements of the sliding option were better than the hinging structure, the application faced problems with the limitation of the area that was available for PV cells, the movement of the membrane and the water tightness of the roof. Therefore we had to leave the idea of a continuous kinetic surface following the path of the sun.

Instead we developed a double-layered load-bearing kinetic tensegrity structure with a stable tensile structure in the upper layer. The lower part of the tensegrity grid is kinetic and has the capability to move in the x and y axis by means of a four-"bar" linkage system. Because the bars in the four bar linkage system are under tension they have been replaced by cables. The vertical struts make a field of height points in the membrane surface. They will be able to hinge in all directions. The connection of the membrane and strut is made by a ball hinge at the height points of the membrane. The rotating struts punch through the membrane roof at the hinging point. On top of the bars, a PV cell is connected that will follow the path of the sun by the hinging of the struts.

We made several digital and physical models and a prototype of a roof structure. To allow the free movement and adjustment of the cables we developed several special details.

tensegrity

Within a tensegrity system, continuous tensile members and discontinuous compressive members form a state of equilibrium. Three different cable types will cope with the tensile forces, while the struts deal with the compression forces. The externals structure, i.e. compression ring, will compromise the total inward forces of the system.

The word 'tensegrity', invented by Buckmister Fuller, is a combination of tension and integrity. The first-known three-dimensional tensegrity system is the one by Ioganson in 1920. He made a stable structure of three bars and nine strings. Because the bars did not contact each other, it is a so-called first-class tensegrity system. Tensegrity or tensegrity-like structures have been used in architecture for circular roofs. The first dome was designed by Fuller and is called after him. The domes have a triangle deviation of tensile strings and vertical bars within a circular compression ring. Geiger improved Fuller's design by changing the triangular grid into a rectangular grid. In the Geiger dome, loads are carried from a central tension ring through a series of radial ring cables, tension hoops and intermediate diagonals.

In 1960, Snelson designed a tensegrity structure with a tension and compression form similar to woven fabric. Between 1998 and 2000 Motro et al. made this experimental double-layered grid of about 80 square meters with a weight of 12 kg per square meter. Their challenge was to prove that this structure can be built as easy as a regular space frame. By varying the length of de strings or rods Geiger domes or other tensegrity structures can be made kinetic, like the movable mast created by Frei Otto in 1976.

kinegrity

In 2014 a new kinetic tensegrity system was developed with a stable tensile structure as top layer of the double-layered grid. The lower cable grid has the capability to move in the x and y axis and therefore the vertical bars can hinge in all directions. These bars will make a field of highpoints in the membrane surface. At these height points the bars will punch through the membrane roof and the hinging point is at the height point of the stable tensile roof structure. On top of the bars a PV cell is connected that will follow the path of the sun by the hinging of the vertical bars. The struts and the cables form a two way frame of bowstring-girders in the x and y axis. The hinging points of the girders are on the horizontal axis of the bowstring-girders. The struts in a bowstring have a varying length that will result in a non-parallel linkage. A parallel linkage would be desired and to minimize the deviation between the struts it is important to minimize the relative difference in length between the struts. For the structural behaviour of the tensegrity it is better to maximize the difference in length. In the design roof structure below we tried to find a compromise between the two contrary demands knowing that a misalignment of 10 degrees for the PV panels would be acceptable. It is of importance that the hinging highpoints are in a plane surface. In this way the hinging points of the highpoints are on the hinging line of the bowstring. It makes that the total length of the cables is always the same during the movement of the structure. Because of this, a lens configuration is not desired and will give friction in the kinetic behaviour of the structure.

A two-way bowstring without bracing has no stability. The pre-stressed membrane structure hanging on the supported high points is anchored to the ground and has to give stability to the structure. The dome shape of the tensile structure has a positive effect on the wind load of the complete structure.

The benefits of a kinegrity solar tracking textile roof structure are:

- PV cells will be used in the most optimal way as a result of the dual axis solar tracking system.
- This system is also able to collect solar energy in the early morning, late evening and winter.
- The structure might also be used in façades, but roof structures are preferred because for roofs there are fewer demands as façades and have in most cases a better orientation to the sun.
- Tensegrity structures are one of the most optimized structural typologies for making large-span roof structures and add an architectural value to the building.
- The structure uses a minimum of material sources compared to other roof structures and solar tracking systems.
- The integration of an architectural roof structure with a dual-axis solar tracker is cheaper than a membrane roof and a solar tracker separately.
- The PV cells will give shadow on the membrane roof and will therefore have a positive effect on the cooling capacity of the building below the membrane structure.
- This solution will provide the local production of electricity for direct use and therefore save on net work systems for the transportation of electricity.
- The solution is completely demountable and recyclable.

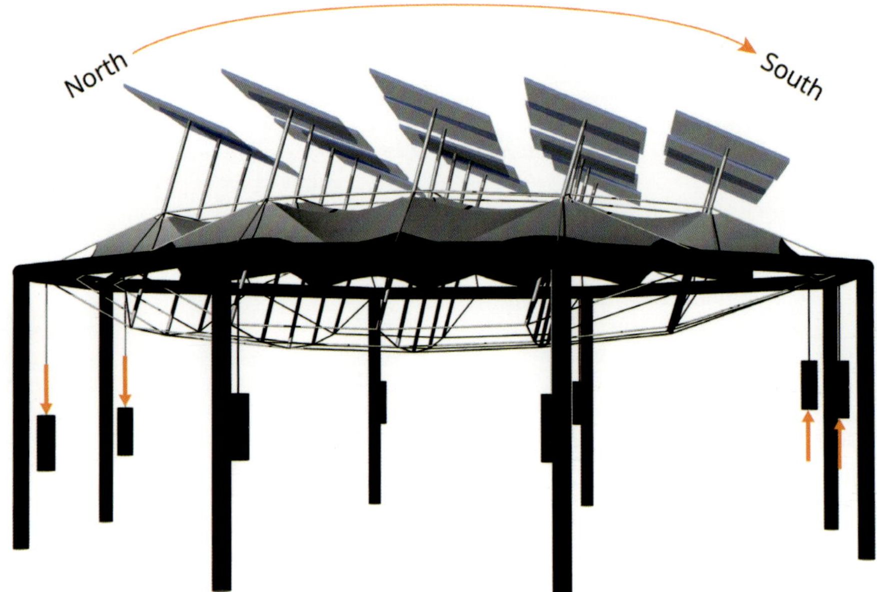

west view of kinetic tensegrity with dual solar tracker

prototyping

By using the visual programming tool Grasshopper, parametric models are developed to create, analyse and compare a wide variation of configurations. With the help of springs, a component within the Kangaroo plug-in, lines are turned into spring elements which can simulate both the axial forces of pre-tensioned cables and the stiffness compressive elements. Beside the analytical research, all situations have been tested by making models and prototypes. Through physical modelling a better understanding of kinegrity structures is obtained whereby specific details and system configurations could be developed for an optimal working prototype. During the research a variation of physical models has been developed, from small illustrating scale models to full scale and test models.

detailing

Tensioning of the total kinetic system within the prototype is realised by hanging weights on all ends of the bottom cables. This simple solution is perfect for the research purposes because the precise applicability and the possibility to cope with length changes for hinging of the struts.

Using counterweights, the axial forces within the system are controlled for hinging; only the resistive forces from the system need to be compromised. Specific details are developed for the reduction of the resistive forces to lower the energy impute for a maximum efficiency. By using bearing pulleys, the resistance of the bottom cable guidance to the hanging weights is reduced to a useful level. Thereby, these pulleys are the connection and the transfer of forces from the kinegrity system to the external structure. This connection needs to be fully flexible to cope with the changing directions of the cables.

The cable to strut connection is of significant influence on the total hinging resistance, thereby price; complexity and functionality are the determining factors that need to be considered. The developed detail for the prototype is simple, cheap and easy to use. Thereby, it minimizes the momentum force in the hinge point, which counteracts the hinging movement. The momentum is determined by the width of the connection; the connection, or turning point, has to be as small and as close to the strut centre as possible.

While the struts punch trough the membrane to support and angle the PV-cells, they need to transfer the upward force, generated in the bottom cables, to the membrane to reach an equilibrium state of the system. These connection points between the membrane and struts are the hinging points, which need to allow the membrane itself to be static while it generates a minimum amount of resistive forces. To cope with the complexity of these multiple problems, a high point detail is developed which connects the membrane and the struts through ball joints. The membranes' clamps are pressed in the form of the joint bowls while on the struts a perfect ball is mounted.

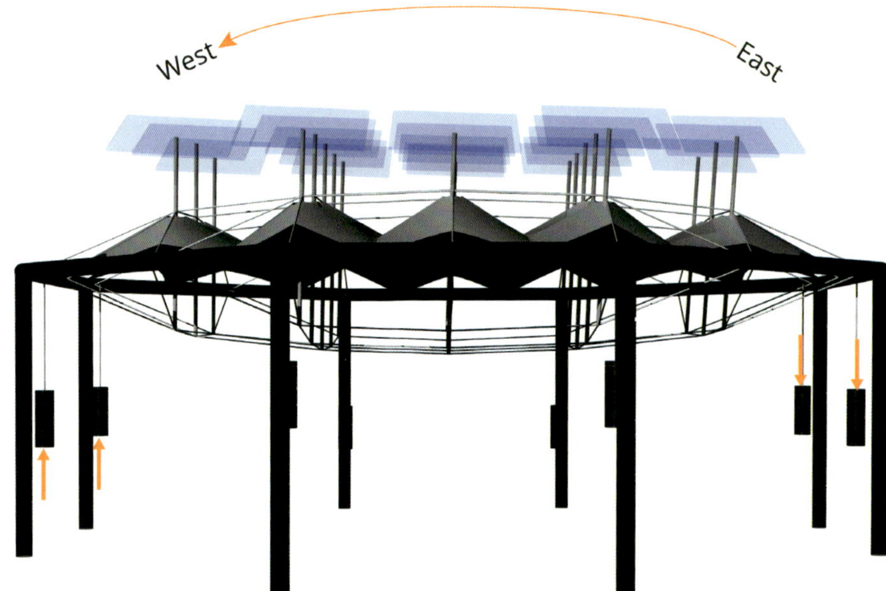

south view of kinetic tensegrity with dual solar tracker

conclusion

A kinegrity is a load-bearing tensegrity structure that has the ability to be kinetic. Kinegrity structures do not have to be deployable. Deployable tensegrity structures might be seen as kinegrities but have a focus on the unfolding of prepared packages to a fixed position. In this case we used a kinegrity as a sun tracker. Other applications for kinegrity structures might be found in the sun shading of facades, for acoustics and for structural adaptation of non-permanent load cases. In this case the structure has a double layer. The upper layer is not kinetic and therefore it is possible to realise this layer as a folded surface in fabric. The combination of a load-bearing tensegrity structure, kinetic behaviour of a double-axis sun tracker, and continuous membrane roof is complex and determines the design possibilities. The system developed can find its application in big-span lightweight roof structures.

acknowledgement

We thank Staalconstructiebedrijf Schuurmans VOF, St.-Lambertusstraat 34/A, 5266AE, Cromvoirt, the Netherlands, Carpro, Industriezone Rovert Gewerbestrasse 36, B-4731 Eynatten, Belgium, the staff of SID and Vanmussenboek laboratorium of the TU/e and the Master students Built Environment: T.A.H. Nieuwenhof, W.A. Schuurmans and S.H.C. Zwarts. Without their input and collaboration it was impossible to realize this research and project.

references

Boer, B. (2012) Climate adaptive building shells. In: *Conference proceedings of the 7th Energy Forum, solar building skins, Bressanone, 2012.*

Calledine, C. R. (1978) Buckminster fuller's "Tensegrity" structures and Clerk Maxwell's rules for the construction of stiff frames. *Solid structures*, 14, pp 161-172.

Connely, R. and Back, A. (1988) Mathematics and Tensegrity. *American scientist*, 86.

Cooke, D. (2011) Single vs dual axis solar tracking, *alternate energy eMagazine.*

Drew P. and Otto, F. (1976) *Form and structure.* Colo: Westview Press, Boulder.

Goetzberger, A., Hebling, C. and Schock, H. (2002) Photovoltaic materials, history, status and outlook *materials science and engineering.*

Herzog, T., Minke, G. and Eggers, H. (1976) *Pneumatic structures: a handbook of inflatable architecture.* Oxford Press.

Knight, F.B. (2000) *Deployable antenna kinematics using tensegrity structure design.* Florida: University of Florida.

Raducanu, V. and Motro, R. (2001) *Composition structurale de systèmes de tenségrité.* Société de Tissage et Enduction Serge Ferrari.

Raducanu, V. and Motro, R. (2001) *Système constructif et architecture: cas des systèmes de tenségrité.* Contrat SLA/LMGC/Ferrari, rapport final.

Snelson, K. (1988) The art of tensegrity. *International journal of space structures*, 27.

Telgen, M. V. van. (2012) *Parametric design and calculation of circular and elliptical tensegrity domes.* Eindhoven: Master thesis, Technical University Eindhoven, Structural engineering.

Tibert, A. G. and Pellegrino, S. (2003) *Deployable Tensegrity Masts AIAA.* Norfolk VA.

parsons design workshop 2014

mark kanters | students: jelisa blumberg, danielle bowler, derick brown, felipe colin jr, kristina cowger, jo garst, jennifer hindelang, mark kanters, mochi liu, sabrina plum and prescila romano emmanuel oni, alexander valencia

Eindhoven University of Technology has been involved in a four year trans-atlantic exchange program called the *Atlantis Program: Urbanisms of Inclusion* through which several students from the TU Eindhoven, KU Leuven and IUAV Venice have been send out to study at Parsons the New School for Design in New York City. It is in this context that I joined the design team of the Parsons Design Workshop 2014.

The Parsons Design Workshop is a graduate architecture studio that provides pro bono design and build services to non-profit organizations. This year, it began its fourth year in a five year partnership with the New York City Parks Department. The Parks Department chose the Sunset Park Recreation Center and Pool in Sunset Park, Brooklyn as the site where the Design Workshop would intervene. Currently, the interior of the recreation center is converted into locker/changing rooms during the swimming season, which means that the center's activities cannot continue during the summer months. The students in the Workshop were tasked with the creation of two new pavilions for changing and locker rooms. The new pavilions will provide 240 square meter of usable area, so the interior programs can operate year round and these community services can continue undisrupted.

During this workshop I experienced the design process from conception to realization. With a team of ten students we spent the four-month spring semester designing, and the three-month summer semester building our design. We attended client meetings with the Parks Department and considered their demands for the operation of the building. We presented to community boards and considered their opinions. An important challenge we overcame was the presentation to the Landmarks and Preservation Commission, where we presented to the commission and received their approval to build adjacent to a New York City Landmark. These milestones were part of the design process and created a learning environment where we learned by doing. Decisions were made as a team: developing the 100.000 dollar material budget, calculating the structural loads, ordering materials, planning construction, and managing public relations. All of this went into the design.

While other academic projects might only exist on paper, this was a learning experience that continued on the construction site. The summer construction months proved that the design process continues on the job site: earlier mistakes had to be resolved and actual materials sparked new inspiration and insight. Building the pavilions with the tools and the perspective of a construction worker generated valuable learning moments for us as students. As we became more comfortable with the tools we became more aware of possible design solutions. Doing the construction work itself inspired an ongoing questioning of the design which is a valuable experience for any architecture student: rethinking and refining the various possible ways how things may be put together, as long as it takes to find the ultimate makeable elegant solution.

finished men's changing pavilion

danielle operating the hydraulic hammer on the bobcat, breaking up the concrete deck

mochi bending the rebar in position, ready for the concrete poor

completed roof structure on both pavilions

the fringe, celebrating the exception

juliette bekkering | graduation project fouad addou

Architecture essentially comes into being between two contrary conditions: architecture of the city versus natural refuge. The studio's assignment is to create a natural refuge within the heart of the city.

By researching and analyzing forgotten locations, border zones, marginalized and leftover areas these 'areas of friction' can be charted. These very areas of friction are favorable locations where new urban functions, special activities and new urban life and uses can be established. These leftover/marginal areas (fringe zones) have specific characteristics and exist under uncommon conditions which are often forgotten, undeveloped and marginalized. The negative aspects which come with these location make many prevailing architectonic solutions unsuited for application here. These locations demand new ideas and design solutions.

The assignment of the graduation studio "the fringe" concerned three core concepts: sculpture, scenography and structure. These three concepts are derived from Vitruvius' three basic architectural ideas (firmitas, utilitas, venustas – that is, solid, useful, beautiful) and each play a leading and ever-changing role in architecture theory, for example in Le Corbusier's book "Vers une Architecture" where he unravels and reinterprets these concepts into volume, plan, and surface.

For this assignment the concepts of sculpture, scenography and structure were employed as a design method in order to develop an architecture with multiple layers of meaning: at the level of architecture as object in its context (sculpture), architecture that creates space and spaciousness (scenography), and the material and materiality of architecture (structure).

Sculpture here refers to the balance between the manifest form and the urban and cultural context such as how buildings fit into their environment and how this is expressed.

Scenography here refers to the typology and spatial organization of buildings. This includes not only how to design a functional plan, but also the experience of architecture, spatial structure, how to determine how spaces feel and sound, how to organize functions, and which (new) uses this can generate.

Structure concerns the manipulability of the building and how its structure, technical aspects, construction, detailing and materiality can be mobilized as expressive design instruments.

literature search

A literature search was conducted in conjunction with the design inquiry. Three books were read and analyzed in order to give the design as an activity a deeper interpretation and cultural context: "A Scientific Autobiography" by Aldo Rossi , "Delirious New York" by Rem Koolhaas and "The Craftsman" by Richard Sennett.

Although these books may appear to have little to do with one another, close examination reveals that they do share a connection as the three central themes of the books relate to the central themes of the studio: sculpture, scenography and structure.

Aldo Rossi's book takes the reader on a search for his personal motives behind design. "Delirious New York" describes the power of programming within architectonic design. Richard Sennett's "The Craftsman" addresses the relation between division of labor, quality of life, and craft.

These three themes are brought together in a series of essays on various subjects. In a detailed research and analysis section these three aspects are further unraveled, examined and brought together.

This book constitutes the results of a year-long search by thirteen students for tools to give meaning to creative architectonic design.

location

The graduation studio took place on Stvanivce island in the middle of Prague in the Vltava riverbed. The Vltava meanders through the city and has determined the city's form to a large degree. The river contrasts starkly with the city: a surprising mass of water with green islands like small natural oases, and a (sometimes swelling, sometimes shrinking) river which changes form each season, sometimes flowing slowly with small patches of speed, but when it really rains it swells, bursting its banks. Islands and quays flood and the river with its islands and banks becomes impassable. These annually recurring floods – sometimes quite heavy – have ensured that the city turned away from the river and the left the islands, banks and washland only poorly accessible, lost green oases in the heart of the city.

the assignment

The assignment of the design studio "The fringe, celebrating the exception" was to put together a design proposal for a building on Stvanice island in the Vltava river in the heart of Prague. Students were told to take a position vis-à-vis the role of the island as a "fringe" area in the city and to formulate a vision of how its qualities could be reinforced.
A program needed to be formulated for the building which deepened the contrast: "retreat in nature" versus "architecture of the city". This program had to provide a place for a new identity and make sense in relation to the nearby historic city center.

Together the students formulated a supplementary, second program to be integrated into the building by each participant as a contrasting element to their self-chosen primary program. The theme chosen was: contemplation. Each student was able to develop a specific program for this component: a library, a chapel, a quiet center, or a spacious loft.

Divided into three groups, we developed three plans for the island. These three urban plans all contained a general, ordering element which structured the plan, organized its construction, and formulated a vision for how to deal with the flooding.

What follows are the results of the individual efforts, how the design fits into its context, the spatial organization of the design, and the elaboration of the design in material and detail.

2. an architectural refuge on an isolated island in the city center

exemplary project

Fouad Addou's project 'Dom-ino vs. the Cave' illustrates the essence of this studio. First, it offers a new interpretation of the fringe area in Prague and activates it with an expressive architectonic solution. Fouad describes his point of departure as follows: "The expansion of cities is happening at the cost of natural environments and is resulting in a deficit of areas that function as a retreat from stressful metropolitan lifestyle. City life is full of stimuli, such as technology and New Media, that help people live their lives more efficiently but prevent them from focusing on life itself. The architecture of the fringe should support the role of refuge and not destroy it through traditional urbanization. This graduation project takes up the challenge to provide a refuge from the stressful contemporary urban condition and uses architectural means to create a platform for individual self-reflection and joint reflection about the impact of new media technology." (fig. 2)

sculpture

The design's main feature is a cut through the heart of the island in order to create a deeply set public space. This cut, made from concrete, works as an ordering element, protects locals from the threat of high water, and leaves the green oasis around it intact (this was one of the common urban design ideas). Fouad employs a cinematic method of dramatic transitions and opposites between spaces which makes the experience of the whole a contemplative process and simultaneously reinforces the psychological dis-

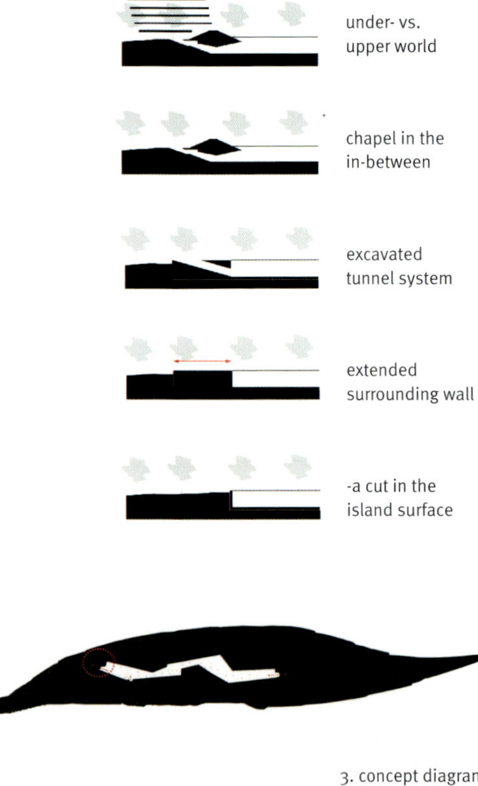

3. concept diagrams

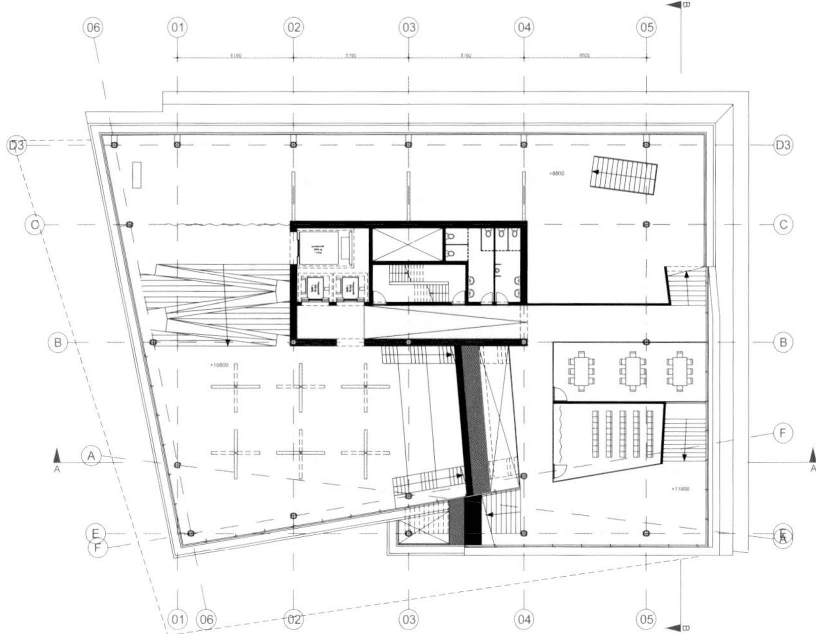

4. 3rd floor new media museum

tance which characterizes the fringe. Fouad describes this process as follows:

"From inside the cut people experience a dramatic inaccessibility and discrepancy towards the island and city around it. High concrete walls surrounding the space and the lowered undulating surface between them give a feeling of otherworldliness. To arrive in the upper parts of the building people have to cross a series of tunnels. The transparent upper parts work as a vertical boulevard that ends with a view over the treetops toward the city and liberates the people from the inaccessibility they have experienced." (fig. 3)

scenography

Two elementary, yet opposite, design principles ensure a contrast of spatial character between what Fouad calls a 'metaphoric upper and lower world'. The upper world is a reinterpretation of Le Corbusier's 'Dom-ino principle' and is here used in order 'to create a continuous vertical boulevard of openness and flexibility for the New Media Museum (fig. 4).' 'The New Media Museum consists on one hand of a publically accessible route for oration and education in order to represent the material and tangible aspects of new media, and on the other hand of an exposition space which represents its digital and intangible aspects. Together the routes represent the parallel existence of an immanent virtual world alongside a physical world'.

The lower world is a reinterpretation of the 'enclosed space' described by theorists such as Bruno Zevi, Luigi Moretti, Collin Rowe and Robert Venturi; it can be seen in the spaces of the lower world which appear to have been excavated from solid rock. In this way, 'intimacy and drama are created via disassociation from the external appearance of the upper world for the chapel.' A similarly formed tunnel must be crossed in order to reach the New Media Museum. 'In combination with the lower world, this tunnel serves to purify the spirit before and after it is bombarded by the impulses of the New Media Museum' (fig. 1).

Fouad's graduation thesis "provides an approach to the inevitable urbanization and development of fringe areas. It ensures that the metropolitan citizen preserves a place of refuge from the stress of city life and responds to an important social issue through a poetic and unconventional way of architectural storytelling. By re-interpreting existing building principles it finds a balance between the architecture of the city and retreat from the stress it can bring."

conclusion

During the course of the graduation studio each student developed their own instrumentarium and design methodology with which they will tackle the most diverse design assignments as a future architect. If graduation can be seen as a quest, a voyage of discovery, during which a basis is laid for an architectonic vocabulary, then this quest has reached its conclusion – for now.

tunnel entrance of the 'big dig', project in the center of boston photographed by willem schilte. the previously on ground level located highway was sunken into the ground, eliminating a barrier and creating space for development and connections.

move = innovating and rethinking existing protocols for moving

architecture of smart mobility
towards an architectural language for new, smart concepts of mobility

franz ziegler and pieter van wesemael | graduation project guido litjens

We studied two cities exemplary for their optimistic attitude toward mass transport and car mobility: the city of Eindhoven (NL) and Boston (USA). As concerns Boston, we looked at the heritage of the urban landscape projects of Frederic Law Omlstead and his heirs in the "Park Movement" and the later "Highway Movement." We studied the iconic Boston Park system and its partial destruction in the sixties by the Business District Developments (CBD) with multilevel highway systems. Finally we analyzed the renovation of downtown Boston after the construction of the massive underground highway tunnels of the so-called "Big Dig," creating valuable new public space (in the spirit of Olmstead) on top of the infrastructure. By doing so Olmstead's Emerald Necklace was extended with a Green Necklace above the Big Dig and a Blue Necklace along the coastline of Little Italy.

Our premise is that our modern society, our way of living and our habitat is largely dependent on our ever-increasing mobility and mobile lifestyles. But clearly our view of mobility, specifically auto-mobility, has become critical and problematic in recent decades. Mobility is a phenomenon increasingly perceived in negative terms of pollution, noise, traffic jams, stress, deadly accidents, and unsustainability, consuming a wide variety of our scarce raw materials. Thus our view of mobility is increasingly critical.

This is even more true when it comes to the infrastructural spaces we create: motorways, rail networks, dedicated bus lanes, etc. These are vast worlds of their own with what most consider extremely negative features: a technocratic space of concrete, asphalt and steel unpleasant and unhealthy to be in and only endured as a means to get to better places.

French urban anthropologist Marc Auge considers the highway as a non-place, a space of transience without any socio-cultural significance, as opposed to streets, parks and squares of the traditional city or the lanes, riverbanks, woods and estates of the countryside. Highways are an infrastructural world which we clearly do not perceive or value as part of the public domain or our habitat. On the contrary, until the nineteen-seventies the infrastructure world was seen as an extremely positive and constructive new technology emancipating and liberating all of us, enabling us to leave the industrious city and live in the more peaceful rural suburbs, commute to work, shop on Saturdays and take a trip on Sundays. Metro lines and grand public transport master plans were celebrated and integrated with large scale urban renewal programs. Mobility created its own world, but this was still an integral part of the public domain of the city and countryside. It was not only a place of transience but a destination, a very habitable one with its own culture.

In those days "mobility landscapes" were enthusiastically designed by architects and urbanists developing and inventing a whole new architectural language - special typologies and aesthetics for the mobile city. This resulted in a whole new gamut of drive-in and -through multi-layered building typologies for the strip, the suburb and the city center. Think of Boston's civic center where atrium, plaza and parking garage are ingeniously stacked into an subtle system of streets, terraces and squares forming a habitable forum for the heart of the city.

This interest on the part of architects and urbanists in the new world of (auto-)mobility is clearly reflected in the manifestoes star architects made during the late nineteenth and twentieth centuries: from Olmsted and Henard, through Le Corbusier and Wright, along Rudolph, Kahn, the Smithons to our own Dutch masters such as Bakema and van Eesteren. Unfortunately for at least the last 30 years the domain of infrastructure and mobility has been neglected and not been part of the architectural debate. Our studio revisited and analyzed the famous infrastructural projects of the nineteen-thirties and nineteen-sixties in order to fuel a new discourse on this very relevant and urgent field.

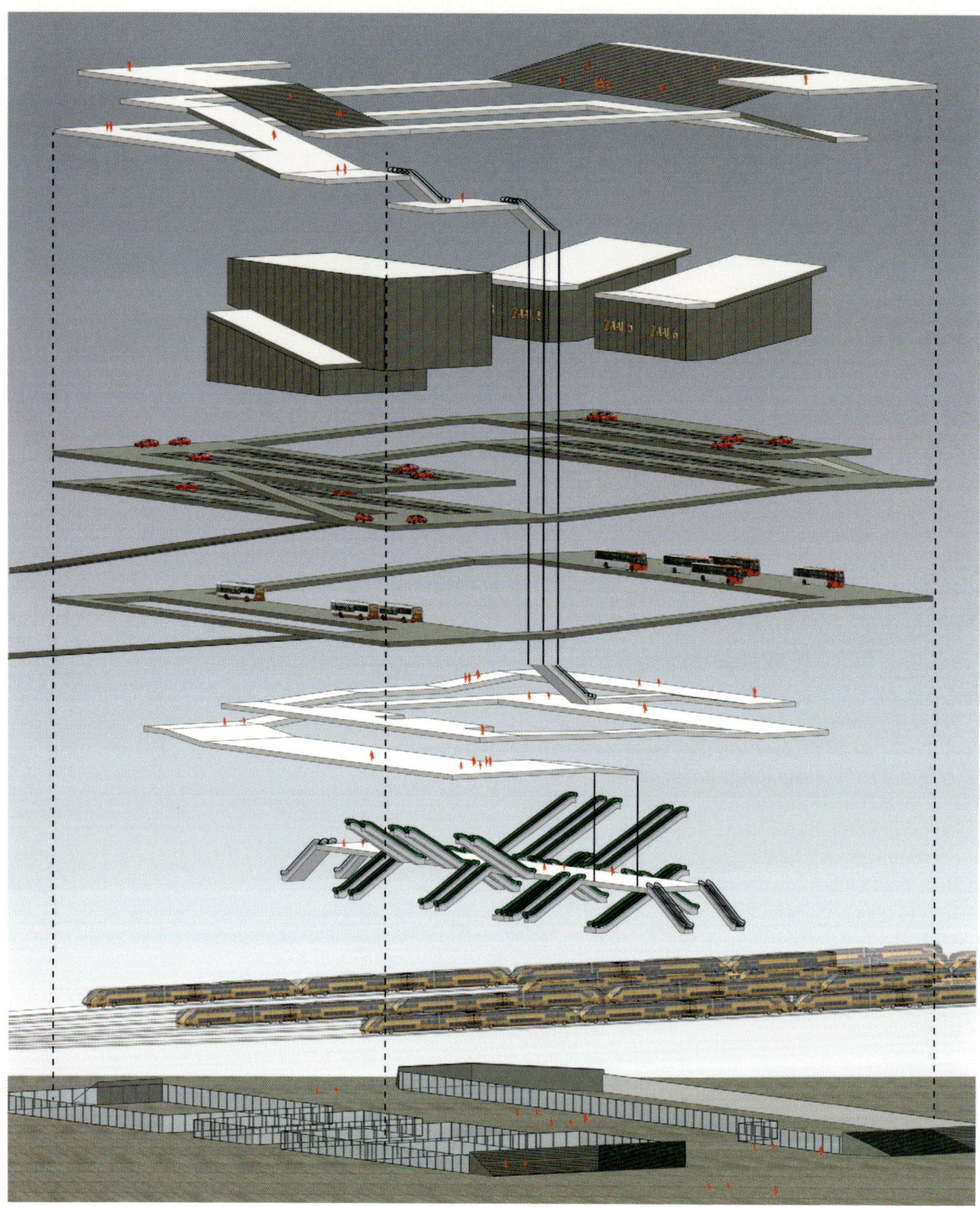

exploded view of functions

exemplary project

Eindhoven is perhaps the most car-oriented city in the Netherlands thanks to one of the leading Dutch urbanists of the early twentieth century - de Casseres - who turned Eindhoven into a lab for urban planning. After World War Two renovation of a large part of the city's infrastructure was inspired by the ideas of the American Parkway Movement but executed in a more moderate version: less park and more road. Also in Eindhoven Central Business District Developments created a lot of non-places in and around the historic center. In Eindhoven as well as Boston there is a need for repairing the accidents - the non-places.

section

Guido Litjens took on the challenge of transform-
ing one of the most complex non-places and one of
the most challenging mobility typologies: the train
station between the old city center and the Fellenoord
Parkway. The train station typology has gone through
an amazing development since the first examples were
built in the nineteenth century. The train station has
been loaded with an incredible set of contemporary
functions. We now have new names for train stations
such as "Transferium" or "Multimodal Hub." The real
function of these complex buildings is to offer smooth
transition from one mode of transport to another
for masses of people. The need for massive capacity
makes the spatial design of these type of buildings
highly challenging. Furthermore, the commercial
spinoff this program requires demands an even
smarter design. One can say that the train station has
been connected to the bus station, the parking lot,
bicycle parking, the metro station and on top of that
cross-bred with a commercial mall, a multiplex theater
and other leisure programs. Guido has defined this
challenge as "designing a city within a city."

In recent years we have seen new interest in Architecture and Mobility. The most urgent challenge of
redesigning the main train stations in the Netherlands
is under construction. The IABR 2014 (Internationale
Architectuur Bienale Rotterdam) showed how the
expert office Benthum and Crouwel have redesigned
central stations in Amsterdam, Rotterdam, Utrecht

and The Hague. Guido has analyzed these redesigns
and relates them to earlier iconic projects like Grand
Central Terminal New York (1913), Euralille (1994) and
Berlin's Hauptbahnhof (2006). These projects offer
a fascinating reference and vocabulary to explore. We
can see that these projects reintroduce the monumental public space so often missing in the modern city.

Guido's project for Eindhoven Central 2.0 can be read
of as a critique of the current development of Eindhoven's Central Station. In his analyses he reveals the
poor organization of functions and the fragmented
spatial quality. Most spaces are still monofunctional
and coexist with other functional spaces. The design
for the upgrade in the coming years does not change
this fundamentally in order to accommodate the
expected steep rise in travelers visiting this station/
transferium. The even more important challenge is to
really integrate this hub into the public domain of the
city center. An example of this kind of integration is
Grand Central Terminus in New York which is an integral, monumental and very lively part of Manhattan.

The urban intervention Guido has designed is a statement of the serious need to take Eindhoven Central
Station to another level and come face to face with
the full complexity of the requirements ahead. This
statement lies in the special strategy to stack programs vertically and radically integrate them around a
monumental public space. This statement requires an

central hall

architectural vision and a new architectural vocabulary. Having said that, Guido wisely borrowed from his reference projects in New York, Lille and Berlin.

Guido is explicitly refers to OMA's project in Eurallile by quoting the "Piranesian Space" designed and proudly showcased by Rem Koolhaas. When programs are stacked and integrated the need for overview and orientation becomes apparent. This is the fabulous lesson from Grand Central Terminus in New York. But here in the so called "Piranesian space" different modes of transport cross within a building through a monumental public vestibule. In a single void all these crossings are revealed. We can speak of a new type of space that addresses mobility and infrastructure. Koolhaas pushed this concept for the "Gordian Knot" of Lille, paradoxically by referring to Piranesi's etchings of his fantasy prisons.

The central void in Guido's project is certainly monumental and impressive. All levels in his design present themselves and are connected with a spectacular web of escalators. The traveler is seduced to climb high into the building in order to look down over the city and into the void full of transiting people. The bus sta-

tion on the fourth level, high above the train platforms, may be the most speculative proposal. But one cannot deny the fascinating possibilities were Eindhoven to embrace such a daring concept. By stacking all transportation modes Guido is able to give the surrounding space back to the city. On both the south side (towards the old city center) and on the north side (towards the TU/e campus) Guido opens up convincing urban squares where people can meet, eat, drink and sit around enjoying greenery and scenery.

Can we now label this project representative of an "Architecture of Smart Mobility?" Yes, certainly if we read it as a seductive and critical statement of current practice. In a smart way the project combines elements from Grand Central Terminus in New York, Eurallile and Hauptbahnhof Berlin thus drawing on an available architectural vocabulary which is rooted in tradition. Yet this raises another question which brings us back to Koolhaas' reference to Piranesian Space. Guido clearly follows Koolhaas when he emphasizes the horizontal lines in his design. The design of his station represents mobility and seeks any opportunity to highlight this by tracing the lines of movement. Structure and support seem to be absent in this building, all

model

levels seem to be floating in thin air. The architecture is light and weightless so as not to compete with the flows of people and transport vehicles. Guido's project is in line with the ideals and grand narrative of modernity from Le Corbusier to Koolhaas. But when we reexamine Piranesi's etchings another question comes up. Piranesi designed a fascinating labyrinthine space, but he shows us heavy structures and bulky bridges in dark perspectives. The vertical lines of the support systems are emphasized. This is heavy architecture! One wonders whether these images could point to a different expression for an Architecture of Mobility, much more massive and structured than Guido's design. We may need to reexamine Paul Rudolph's and Louis Kahn's monumental work. We need to study the massive Spanish TGV stations by Cruz y Ortiz arquitectos and Raphael Moneo. Maybe Koen van Velzen's Breda station will offer a refreshing alternative. In conclusion, Guido's studies and proposal for the Eindhoven Station 2.0 are a fascinating attempt to design for the challenges of Mobility and Architecture. And above all is it a fruitful attempt to refuel discussion of an Architecture for Mobility again in the professional domains of Architecture and Urbanism.

references

Banham, R. (1971) *Los Angeles, the Architecture of four ecologies*. Londen: Penguin Press.

Conzen, M.P. (1990) *The making of the American landscape, Allen & Unwin*. New York.

Geddes, N.M. (1932) *Horizons*. Boston: Dover Publications, Little, Brown and Company.

Gruen, V. (1973) *Centers for the urban environment: Survival of the cities*. New York: Van Nostrand Reinhold.

Houben, F., et al. (2003) *Mobility: a room with a view*. International Architecture Biënnale Rotterdam: Nai Publishers.

Jacobs, J. (1961) *The death and life of great american cities*. New York: Random House.

Kaijima. (2006) *Made in Tokyo*. Tokyo: Kajima Pubishing Institute co.

Litjens, G. (2014) *Eindhoven Central Station 2.0*. Eindhoven.

Neutelings, W. (1988) De Ringcultuur, *Vlees en Beton*, 10. Gent: Vlees en Beton Publishers.

Petunia, G. et al. (1996) *Frederic Law Olmsted, L'orgine del parco urbano e del parco naturale contemporaneo*. Firenze: Centro Di, UFOs.

Provoost, M. *Asphalt, automobiliteit in de Rotterdamse stedebouw*. Rotterdam: 010 publishers.

Smithon, A. (1983) *AS in DS, an eye on the road*. Delft: Delft University Press.

Tafuri, e.a. (1979) *The American city, from civil war till the New Deal*. MIT press.

graduation project: 'tout est poésie' by femke stout, candle wax object describing its brittle behavior by the interaction between object and hand

sense = enlarging the sensibilities that can be experienced in the built environment

slender high strength steel column laterally supported by glass panes

dennie dierks | graduation project dennie dierks

The key design feature of this glass-steel column is the way the glass panes are connected to the steel bar, namely by sliding steel sleeves to avoid direct stresses to occur in the glass panes due to axial column deformation.

Structural steel is a material that allows for slender columns. However, slender steel columns usually have a low load bearing resistance due to flexural buckling. It is possible to suppress flexural column buckling by adding glass panes. Thus, use can be made of the steel section's squash load, reducing the amount of steel involved and obtaining a highly transparent glass-steel column. In this paper, a new type of slender transparent glass-steel column is proposed, consisting of a high strength steel bar supported in lateral directions by glass panes. Its feasibility is shown experimentally and numerically. It is also proven that the design has sufficient redundancy to allow for the loss of supporting glass panes without a reduction of the load bearing capacity.

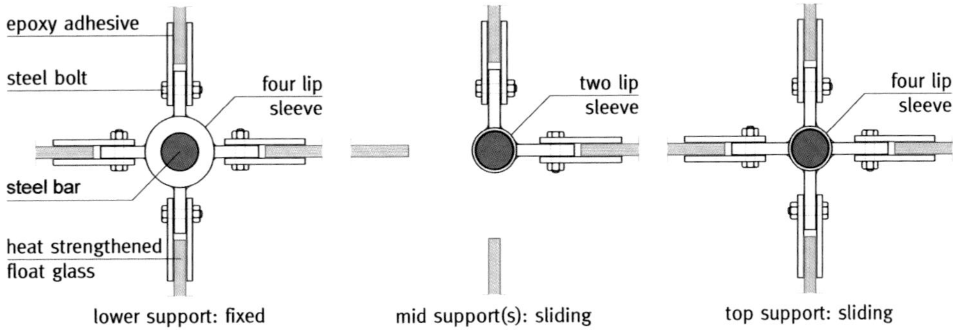

1. cross-sections of the sleeves with two or four glass panes attached

Transparency and slenderness are getting more and more important, as light, openness and reducing visual thresholds are increasingly more central themes in architectural design. Therefore the structural designer has to engineer slender structural elements like columns.

Glass is a material that allows for transparency. In general, glass is a brittle material and therefore special attention has to be paid to safety if it is to be applied as structural element. Several research projects have been carried out to investigate glass columns. They concluded that the end connections are essential elements for proper load introduction.

Structural steel allows for slender columns but the loss of stability through flexural buckling is the dominant failure mode, reducing the load bearing resistance. If flexural buckling is suppressed effectively, the full squash load of the steel column could be achieved.

In view of the architectural qualities glass can offer and the good performance that structural steel has, a glass-steel column where glass panes suppress the occurrence of flexural buckling can be regarded as an excellent structural composite element. A glass-steel column must be designed in such a way that flexural buckling of the steel column is suppressed by laterally supporting glass panes.

If flexural buckling of steel columns can be suppressed effectively and the full yield stress can be utilized, it makes sense to use high strength steel to further reduce the use of material. The present study focussed on the design of a high strength steel bar laterally supported by glass panes, connected by sliding glass-steel sleeve connections to avoid direct stresses to occur in the glass panes. The structural response of the proposed glass-steel column is examined by means of experiments and finite element analyses. Special attention was paid to the loss of one or more glass panes, reducing the number of panes supporting the steel bar, showing the glass-steel column to have sufficient redundancy.

design of the glass-steel column
Eurocode 3 was used as the preliminary design tool and sensitivity analyses using finite element software were subsequently used to further design the glass-steel column. The glass-steel column consisted out of a high strength steel bar with a height of 3600mm, supported by four glass panes with a width of 400mm which were connected by sliding sleeves to the steel bar. Only at the lower support, the sleeve was fixed to the bar. Adhesively bonded stainless steel strips connected the glass panes to the lips welded to the sleeves. Figure 1 shows cross-sections of the column's glass-steel connections. The glass panes are slightly shorter than the height of the steel bar to keep them free from the roof and floor.

Heat strengthened float glass resists a higher maximum principal stress (i.e. tension) than anneal float glass and offers more residual capacity than fully tempered float glass. Therefore, the four supporting glass panes in crucifix arrangement were made of heat strengthened float glass. Using four glass panes, two for each direction, allows losing one glass pane per direction without reduction of load bearing resistance, thus giving the design redundancy.

The most important feature at the finite element simulations was the buckling mode of the glass-steel column. The anticipated flexural buckling mode was buckling locally between the lateral supports (i.e. the sleeves) which only occurred for the clamp-ended glass-steel column. The pin-ended glass-steel column buckled in a global mode. It was therefore decided to design the glass-steel column with clamped ends.

2. impression

3. locally cracked pane test

experiments and simulations

Prior to the full scale tests, small scale tests (tensile, compression and buckling tests) were conducted. The goal of these small scale tests was to obtain material properties, to be used as input data for the finite element simulations. All small scale test specimens were taken from the same steel bar. The full scale test programme consisted of one glass-steel column which was tested four times, changing the number of glass panes for lateral support in each test: Test 1, support by all four glass panes; test 2, support by three glass panes; test 3, support by three and subsequently by two glass panes. Finally, in test 4 the steel bar was tested without lateral support. After testing, finite element simulations were carried out to validate a finite element model for future parametric studies.

Test 1 was terminated at 525 kN to be able to reuse the glass-steel column in subsequent tests. This was similar to the yield stress found in the small scale buckling tests. The finite element simulation reached a load of 526 kN. In test 2 the second highest sliding sleeve seized at 499 kN resulting in a locally cracked glass pane at the top glass-steel connection (3rd picture in figure 3). The finite element simulation reached a load of 495 kN. Test 3 started

with the lateral support of three glass panes. At 314 kN one glass pane failed locally at several glass connections (4th picture in figure 2). Residual lateral support of the locally failed glass panes was assumed to be negligible. Loading was continued up to 520 kN. The finite element simulation reached a load of 519 kN. In test 4 the steel bar started to buckle between 20 and 30 kN. Close to the Euler buckling load of 35 kN of a clamp-ended column the steel bar failed (5th picture in figure 5).

conclusions

It was possible to laterally support a high strength steel bar by glass panes and utilize the steel bar's squash load in tests 1 and 3. Although the squash load was not reached in test 2 it is most likely that the squash load could have been reached if the sliding of the second highest sleeve would have been assured.

The restraining effect (i.e. suppressing buckling) of the glass panes was observed both in experiments and simulations. It was shown that a very slender high strength steel bar can be used as a column if restrained adequately by glass panes. The feasibility of this design was demonstrated.

4. failed pane test

5. buckled column test

In order to avoid direct stresses from occurring in the glass panes, sliding sleeves were used in the design to connect the glass panes to the steel bar and these were shown to be effective.

From test 3 it can be concluded that the steel bar required little lateral support to fully suppress flexural buckling. This test showed that the design has redundancy: two out of four glass panes placed perpendicularly can fail without significantly affecting the load bearing resistance of the glass-steel column.

In order to avoid direct stresses to occur in the glass panes, sliding sleeves were used in the design to connect the glass panes to the steel bar and these were shown to be effective.

recommendations
Concerning the experiments it is recommended to increase the number of glass-steel column specimens. Experimental observations in this paper were based on a single glass-steel column only.

Although it was possible to simulate the tested glass-steel column with sufficient accuracy, it is recommended to further fine tune the FE model based on additional data gained from more experiments. Then, a parameter study to investigate the effect of salient parameters on the failure behaviour of glass-steel columns outside the scope of the experimental programme can be carried out.

Only one glass pane width was used to laterally support the present glass-steel column. Other glass pane widths should be used to investigate the effect of the glass pane width on suppressing flexural buckling.

solarswing© energy

an innovative building-integrated concentrating photovoltaic shading solution

roel loonen, jan hensen, charlotte zhang | graduation project charlotte zhang

Solar©Swing Energy is an innovative building envelope component that combines concentrating photovoltaic (CPV) technology with a dynamic array of advanced optical elements. The façade concept works with innovative lenses that internally trap and redirect sunlight. This optical system treats the diffuse and direct parts of solar irradiation in a different way. The diffuse part freely passes the modules and reaches the room as soft daylight. The direct part, on the other hand, is concentrated onto a tiny solar cell. Because the high intensity-radiation is focused on a small surface, it is a cunning idea to use costly but ultra-high-efficiency PV cells. Doing this gives a boost to overall electrical efficiency at lower cost than conventional crystalline PV surfaces. A dual-axis solar tracking algorithm is used to ensure that the CPV modules are always aligned perpendicular to the sun. Only in this way, the energy production of the fenestration system can be maximized.

a new design solution for glass-covered spaces

solarswing energy in a roof canopy

active and adaptive building skins for zero-energy buildings

All new buildings in the EU have to be energy neutral by the year 2020. Local generation of electricity will become more important as a critical building block towards meeting this *zero-energy* target. All too often, the onsite energy generation happens as an after-thought, manifested in the form of unappealing building-applied photovoltaic panels, or otherwise obtrusive add-on solutions. For truly sustainable solutions, there is a need to develop clever technologies that are more responsive, elegant and efficient, and allow for better integration with the overall building design.

Building skins are positioned at the interface between inside and outside. This is the place where many physical phenomena interact, and energy flows meet. By taking advantage of these exchanges in a more active and dynamic way, building envelopes can play a prominent role in keeping indoor spaces comfortable. In addition, the envelope zone holds endless design opportunities for building-integrated renewable energy production.

The amount of solar energy that impinges on the walls and roofs of buildings is immense. Building designers like to take advantage of the sunlight by including glazed elements, such as atria, conservatories and curtain walls in their projects. It is, however, not only the useful daylight that enters the room; excessive amounts of sunlight may also lead to overheating, increased energy consumption for cooling or ventilation, and can cause visual discomfort in the form of disturbing glare. Solar control strategies, such as blinds, curtains and shutters are often needed to reject solar gains and make up for the negative side-effects of large glazed areas. However, these shading systems require maintenance and may disrupt the striking transparent look-and-feel of a façade. As an additional drawback comes the fact that shading systems are seldom used in an optimal way. Studies show that blinds tend to be lowered most of the time with lights switched on, leaving the occupants with less interaction with the outside world and higher energy bills than necessary.[1-2]

the system remains transparent while it blocks the sun

What if we could harness the power of the solar energy that hits facades and roofs by converting it into electricity, and at the same time provide a shading solution that automatically blocks unwanted direct radiation, yet leaves occupants with a view to outside? This alluring combination of functionalities is exactly the proposition of SolarSwing® Energy.

solarswing® energy

SolarSwing® Energy is an iconic example of a climate adaptive building shell.[3] Actuation of the kinetic CPV modules prevents direct solar radiation from entering the room, providing glare protection where and when needed. A view to outside, and enhanced access to the many health and well-being benefits of daylight [4] is guaranteed at all times. On cloudy days, the bulk of all available light gets transmitted to inside. On sunny days, the diffuse light will still enter, but the more powerful and unwanted direct radiation is effectively blocked and transformed into something useful: electricity.

The multi-functional fenestration concept is designed in modular components to form a prefab design element for double skin facades or glazed roofs. It is an all-in-one solution – no further building envelope components are needed. The electricity that is generated can cover most of the building's energy demand for heating, ventilation and air-conditioning (HVAC) and other plug loads. The development of Solar-Swing® Energy is currently in the prototype phase. More work is needed to bring the concept to the next stage, where it can compete with alternative solutions that are out on the market.

Building performance simulation for product development
The unit Building Physics and Services at the Department of the Built Environment (TU/e) is partnering with SolarSwing® to find the best use for their innovative product. It is our task and research objective in this project to investigate the building-integration opportunities and challenges of the innovative façade component. We support the research and development process through computational modeling and simulation studies from the viewpoint of energy performance and building physics. Among other things, we quantify the performance potential, identify most sensitive system parameters, and on the basis of this, give recommendations for further development of the product design. Building performance simulation (BPS) is our research tool of choice. Over the last few decades, computational BPS models have evolved to become a well-established design support tool in the construction and HVAC design industry. BPS takes into account the dynamic interactions between a building's shape and construction, systems, user behavior and climatic conditions, and is therefore used as a valuable resource in many building design processes. Because of these attributes, BPS can also be used as a tool for supporting informed decision-making in the R&D phase of innovative building envelope components, but such possibilities have only been explored to a limited extent.[5]

Through iterative evaluation of multiple product variants, the integration of simulation allows for strategic decisions that acknowledge high-potential directions in the development process. In our ongoing research,

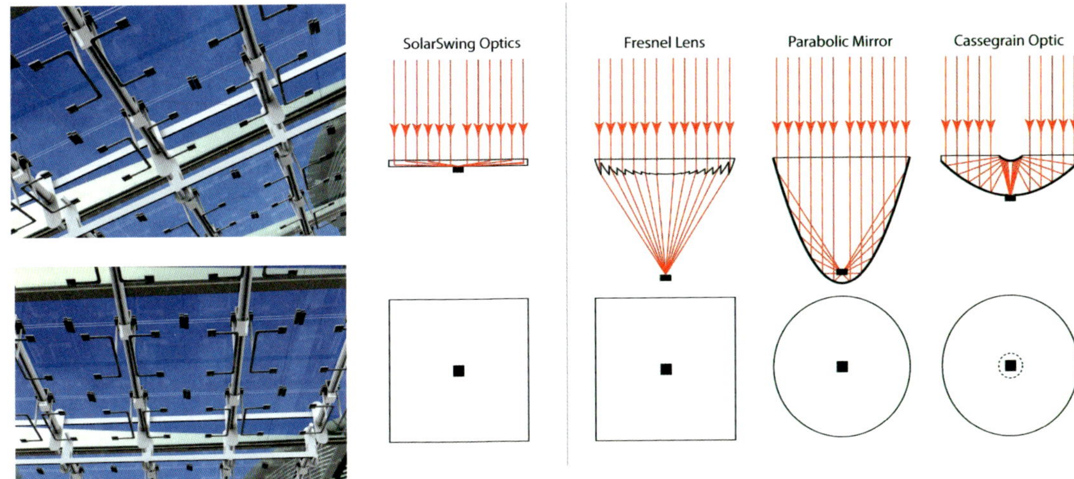

the smart optical system results in a thin module

we try to find answers to the following type of questions:

- What is the energy saving potential of SolarSwing® Energy in terms of heating, cooling and lighting?
- Which comfort aspects are most important? What is the positive contribution to indoor environmental quality?
- How much electricity can be generated, and what is the best configuration of CPV modules to achieve this?
- What is the performance of SolarSwing® Energy in different climate regions? Which location is most promising for the first market introduction?
- Is the technology more promising in residential or in commercial projects?
- Are the benefits of the product sensitive to the different façade/roof orientations?
- Should SolarSwing® focus their efforts on developing one single product, or should they direct their attention to multiple product variants that match better with the needs of different situations?
- Is it possible to harvest the thermal energy that is released from absorption in the CPV modules in a useful way? Can the energy be used for space heating? What about thermal energy storage and system integration?

Initial results of our research show promising results, highlighting that SolarSwing® Energy can lead to zero-energy building operation in many situations. All this information can be used to help formulate the business case for SolarSwing® Energy. Different stakeholders can make quantitative analyses of the various costs and benefits and assess the overall value of the facade system in an objective way. The use of simulation brings some unique elements that cannot be obtained by traditional analysis methods such as mock-ups, experiments or simple calculations. For example, what-if-analyses can be performed ahead of having expensive prototypes, to evaluate the robustness of the new technology in many different usage scenarios and operating conditions. Moreover, BPS can act as a virtual testbed to assess the potential of materials with not-yet-existing properties. All these analyses can be done on the basis of relevant performance indicators, and as such, the method may help creating competitive advantage by improving product performance or time-to-market in a cost-effective way.

references

1. O'Brien, W., Kapsis, K. and Athienitis, A.K. (2013) Manually-operated window shade patterns in office buildings: A critical review. *Build. Environ.*, 60 (2), pp. 319–338.
2. Bakker, L.G., Hoes-van Oeffelen, E. C. M., Loonen, R. C. G. M. and Hensen, J. L. M. (2014) User satisfaction and interaction with automated dynamic facades: A pilot study. *Build. Environ.*, 78(8), pp. 44–52.
3. Loonen, R. C. G. M., Tr ka, M., Cóstola, D. and Hensen, J. L. M. Climate adaptive building shells: State-of-the-art and future challenges, *Renew. Sustain. Energy Rev.*, 25(09), pp. 483–493.
4. Aries, M. B. C., Veitch, J. A. and Newsham, G. R. (2010) Windows, view, and office characteristics predict physical and psycho-logical discomfort. *J. Environ. Psychol.*, 30(4), pp. 533–541.
5. Loonen, R. C. G. M., Singaravel, S., Tr ka, M., Cóstola, D. and Hensen, J. L. M. Simulation-based support for product development of innovative building envelope components. *Autom. Constr.*, 45(9) pp. 86–95.

the dutch *buitenplaats*
the art of framing escape

gijs wallis de vries | graduation project jan herwarts

This essay discusses the heritage of the 'buitenplaats' as a place to satisfy desires of escape, and reflects on the physical and symbolical inscription of flight lines in architecture.

'Escape' is a central theme in my research. Starting from the assumption that the desire of escape is a very old and still vital factor in architectural design, I explored the concept of the 'flight line' developed by the philosopher Gilles Deleuze, and applied it on architecture as an art of 'framing' escape. I concentrated on the transition of classicism to romanticism, exemplified in the works of G.B. Piranesi (1720 -17780). [1]

1   Wallis de Vries, G. (2014) *Archescape. On the Tracks of Piranesi*. Amsterdam: 1001 Publishers. Id., Piranesi (2012) *Le vedute di Roma. A journey through the Eternal City*. Ede: heritage Editions: Ede.

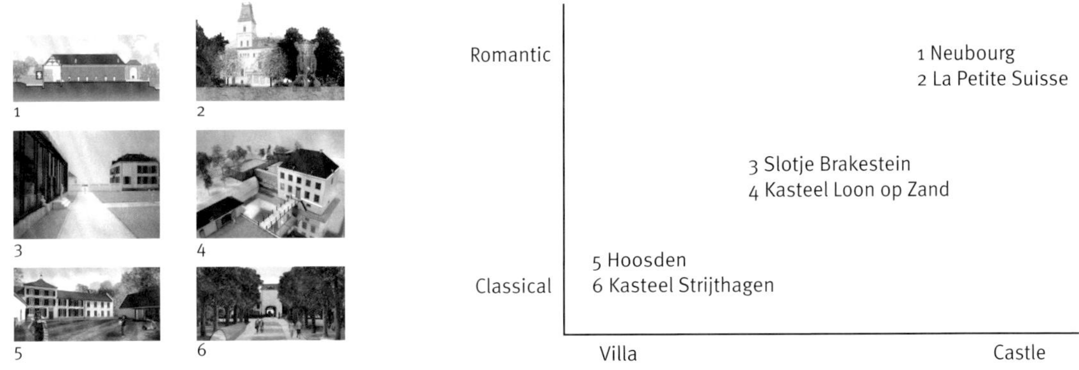

1. diagram of the classical villa and the romantic castle

My interest in 'flight lines' and how architecture 'frames' them, determined the agenda of my Master's seminars and graduation studio, which in their turn stimulated my own research.[2] The research question I proposed to the students of my graduate studio was to find out more about the historical reasons of the Dutch buitenplaats in its relation to the city, particularly in the provinces of Noord-Brabant and Limburg.[3]

Literally translated a buitenplaats (also simply called a 'buiten') is an 'outside place'. Consisting of a country house with gardens for aesthetic and culinary pleasures, a coach house and other outbuildings, it provides an escape from the city. A buitenplaats shapes the landscape it is part of after an Arcadian ideal. In the 17th century, the Golden Age of the Dutch Republic, thousands of buitenplaatsen were founded by merchants and patricians. This tradition continued well into the 20th century. The desire to flee the city and spend leisure time outside changed over the centuries but remains vivid. The relevance of this topic for a graduation studio lies in various fields. Firstly it lies in the opportunity of the recent publication of a guide on the occasion of 'The year of the buitenplaats'[4] that has drawn public attention to a considerable but fairly unknown heritage of Dutch culture. Secondly, it lies in the need to conceive new destinations and possibilities of reuse, requiring new research that fills the knowledge gap between specialized historians and other disciplines. Thirdly, and most importantly, the topical relevance has to do with the field of architecture itself. Indeed, the Dutch buitenplaats embodies a great tradition of villa design that ought to be part of the education of architecture, and must therefore be studied not only by historians but also by designers.

The students participating in this studio discovered the Dutch buitenplaats with delight, and came up with 'out of the box' ideas for a sustainable transformation of its heritage. Largely covering known ground, their research introduced a novel approach by focussing on the architectural question of how to frame flight lines in a leisure landscape. Though situated in the country, the buitenplaats is essentially urban. It expresses the desire to flee the city and regain paradise, satisfied by the art of framing its setting. Painting, poetry, music, and architecture all served the creation of leisure space in the countryside. How was it possible to 'make place' for this paradoxical unity of urban and rural? And what might be its relevance in the age of mass tourism? The students addressed these questions by exploring the history of the buitenplaats, theorizing its themes, and formulating visions. Based on this research every student chose an abandoned or neglected buitenplaats. Different from the northern buitenplaats, usually modelled after the classical villa, buitenplaatsen in the southern provinces are often castles, which, once their military function and position was gone, became dreamy buildings hiding in romantic greenery. In this respect the student's projects can be classified along two axes: from classical to romantic and from the villa to the castle (fig. 1).

2 I reflected on the results of the graduation studio 'Champ de Mars' in 'Framing Landscape', a paper presented at a conference on Landscape and Imagination organized at the Ecole Nationale Superieure d'Architecture de Paris la Villette, published in Newman, C., Nussaume, Y. and Pedroli, B. eds. (2013) *Land scape and Imagination. Towards a new baseline for education in a changing world*. Pisa: UNISCAPE, Bandecchi & Vivaldi, p. 349-352.

3 This graduation atelier resulted in a rich output. Apart from the designs, it consisted of an Atlas, which discusses the research as well as the designs. Shortly after the graduation, on 19 March, the Atlas was presented in castle Heeswijk for a public of stakeholders in the field of buitenplaatsen, who applauded the student projects for their fresh approach. For the young architects, it meant a promising follow-up, which may result in practical involvements, assignments, and at least useful contacts. Besides the Atlas, of which by now some thirty copies have been sold ('printing on command').

4 Dessing, R. W. Chr., and Holwerda, J. (2012) *Nationale gids van de Historische Buitenplaatsen*. Wormerveer: Uitgeverij Noord-Holland.

2. hoosden, aerial view of existing situation

exemplary project

The project of Jan Herwarts for Hoosden exemplifies the whole studio. Not only does it express a creative understanding of the history of the buitenplaats, but it also proposes a consistent theory that answers the question of framing landscape in a setting where rural and urban culture meet. Jan Herwarts himself characterizes Hoosden as follows:

"Veiled by old trees and thick foliage, many hikers will find themselves surprised stumbling upon the house of Hoosden. The old Jesuit buitenplaats has been abandoned for nearly half a century and meanwhile nature has had its way with the buildings. Overgrown and weathered, Hoosden is as romantic as it is intriguing, its serenity bearing witness to its spiritual past. Hoosden consists of a main house and two barns enclosing an intimate courtyard. (fig.2,3) At the eastern side of the main house a terrace overlooks a beautiful field, enclosed by trees. In this sheltered and peaceful environment one can fancy oneself in another world, forgetting about daily life, even if only for a while. In 1940, during his travels through Limburg, W.L. Leclercq described it as a place 'where time is standing still'. It is a prophecy that came true, as it is suggested by the old crates from the 50's and wooden wheelbarrows that are still remaining in the barns."

In his design Jan applied the theory of architectural representation, developed by Ogden and Richards on the basis of the semiotics of Peirce.[5] This theory can be resumed in the 'Triangle of Reference', a triadic relation of sign, concept, and referent (fig. 4). If a buitenplaats represents an Arcadian ideal, what happens if its pleasures refer no more to the wealthy elite, formerly called the leisure class?[6] In order to induce a contemporary social reference Jan proposed the idea of a 'vrijplaats' (free place). He decided that Hoosden should be inscribed in the European network of 'artists in residence', generally located in cities. Hoosden

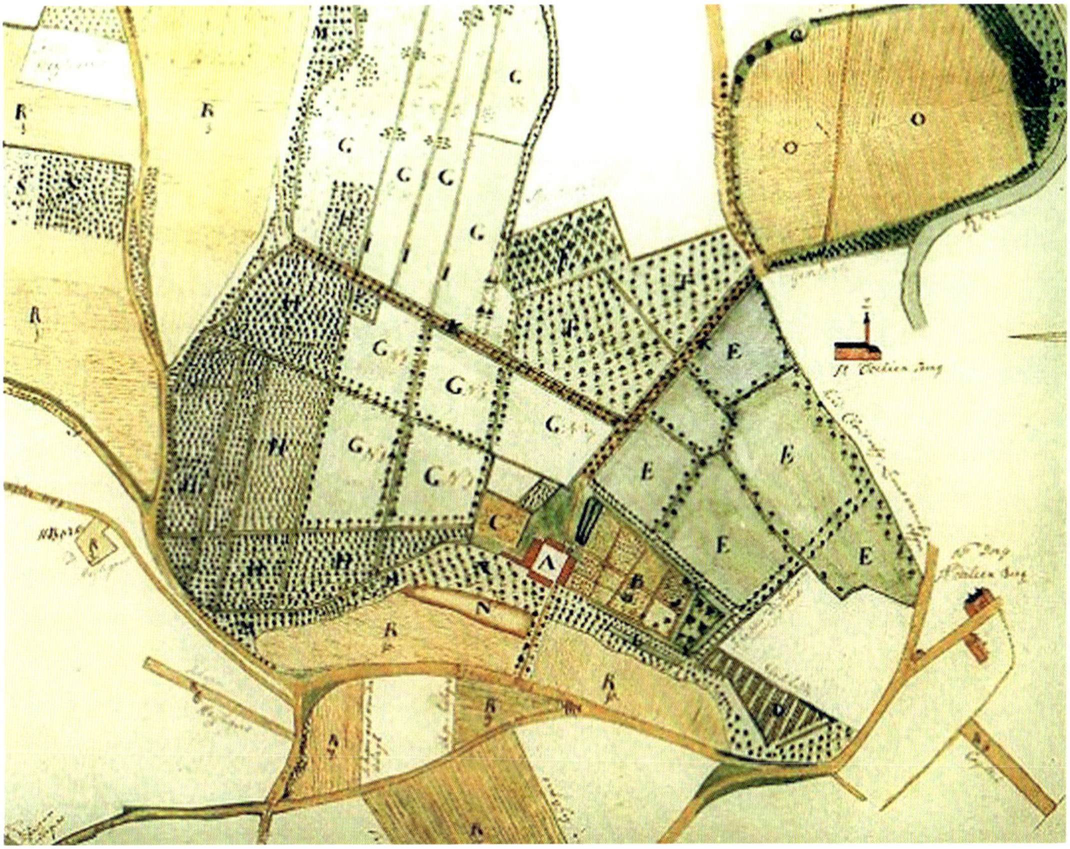

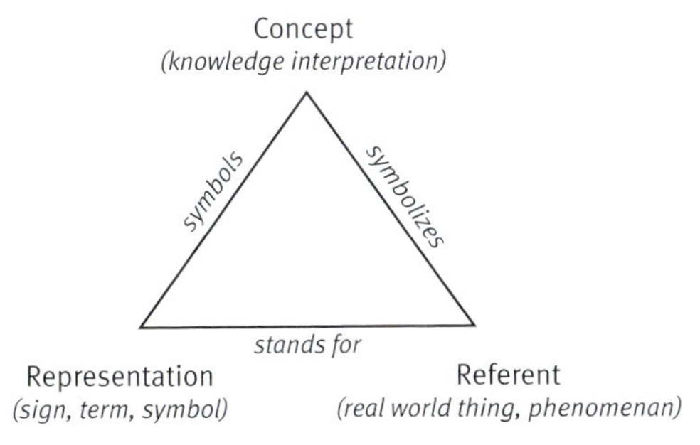

3. historical map

Concept
(knowledge interpretation)

Representation
(sign, term, symbol)

Referent
(real world thing, phenomenan)

4. triangle of reference

would therefore be an exceptional residence, a tranquil and inspiring abode for artists and an enchanting venue for events. Jan explained why Hoosden is suitable for a 'vrijplaats' and how he adapts it as follows:

"Historical maps show that Hoosden is originally composed of a square with a main house and barns, of which today the U-form remains. The main house will once again

5   Jan Herwarts, 'Aanzienlijk decor, Representatie in villa en buitenplaats'('Noble Decor. Representation in villa and buitenplaats'), in Elisabeth Bonavera a.o., *Ongekende Lustoorden. Architectonische atlas van de zuidelijke buitenplaats* ('Unknown pleasure places. Architectural Atlas of the Southern Buitenplaats'), Uitgave TU Eindhoven, maart 2014, p. 54-75.
6   Bentmann, R. and Müller, M. (1992) *The Villa as Hegemonic Architecture.* The authors analyze the representation of the Palladian villa as a dialectical union of opposites: labour and leisure being the crucial one.

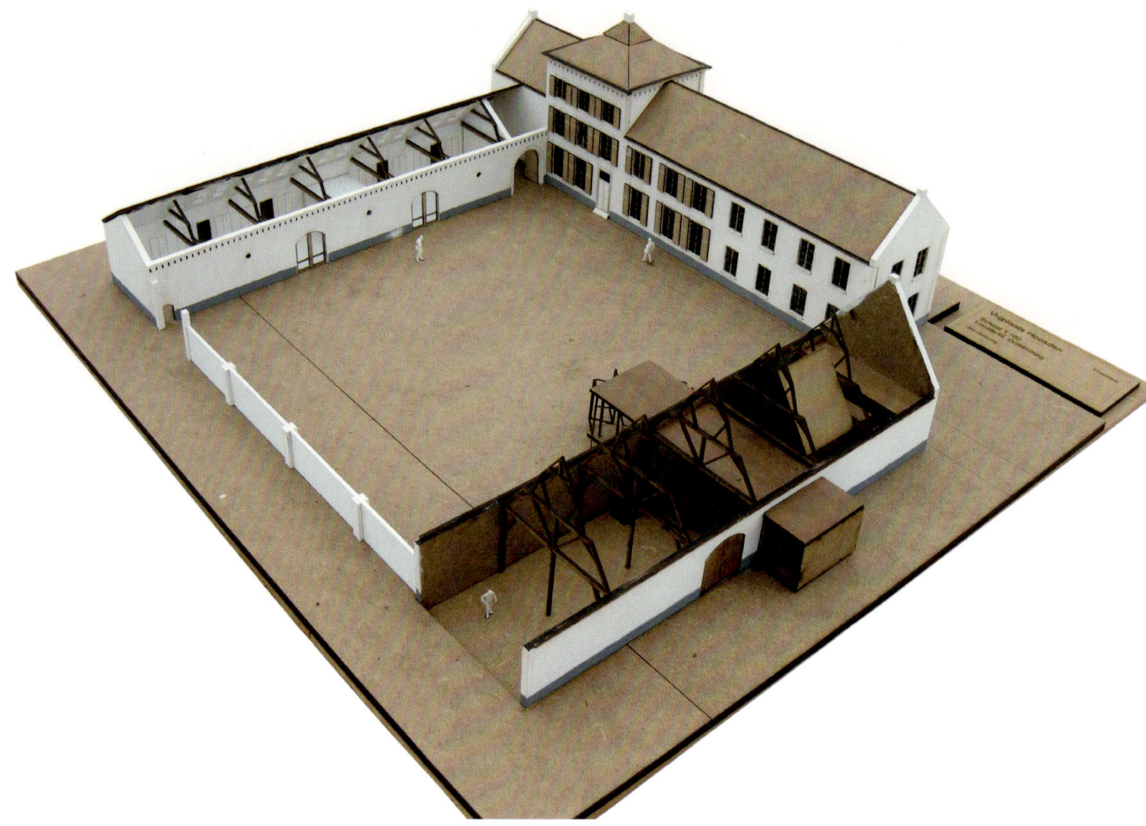

5. vrijplaats hoosden, courtyard, model

serve primarily for living purposes, fitting its prominent position and representative value. By making a few minor changes to the interior, it can facilitate eight studios in which the artists can live and work in private. The northern barn will be rehabilitated as a shared workshop, enabling engagements between the artists as opposed to the private atmosphere in the studios. The southern barn will accommodate a bar, a meeting room and exhibitions, symposia or other festivities (fig. 5). The large space of the barn features a beautiful wooden truss structure and crude brickwork. This rather nostalgic, rural atmosphere will be enhanced by using and reusing the old materials (fig. 6). On summer days the bar fans out onto the courtyard, the heart of the complex. The romantic-fantastic qualities of Hoosden reach a high point in a 'path of imagination', crossing through the wild and exciting swamp forests surrounding the complex. (fig. 7) Along the path several wondrous and estranging follies are designed, challenging the artist to perceive the natural surroundings in a different way. At the same time, the follies play their own part in the rhythm of individual retreat and communal conversation. Each of the follies is a tribute to the traditional follies often found on the buitenplaats."

The programme of the 'vrijplaats' is crystallized in the 'carré' (square) of the main house and adjacent buildings, kept intact and even reinforced, while the slightly angular deviation in the approach is taken further in a 'path of imagination' zigzagging through the park that had become a wilderness. Seemingly disjointed, the free style of the follies placed along its trajectory and the classical renovation of the house nevertheless

6. vrijplaats hoosden, south barn, section

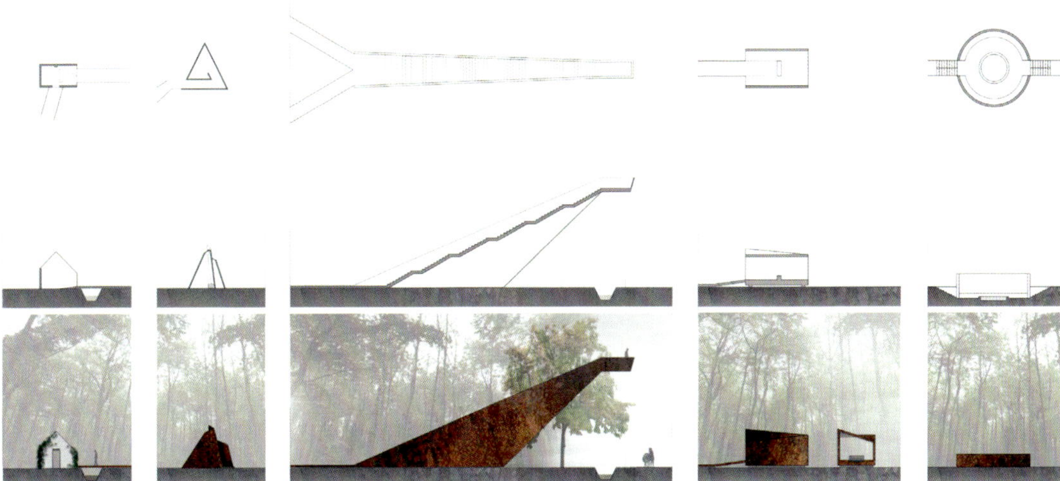

7. vrijplaats hoosden, path of imagination, plan and section with follies

form a coherent whole. Joining spaces for solitary contemplation and for common conversation, the project unites the formal logic of the restored 'carré' with the informal logic of the transformed landscape. It is the art of framing that accomplishes the harmony of the distinct realms. In Martin Heidegger's essay 'Building Dwelling Thinking', he wrote that what makes a place ('Ort') is a quadripartite figure ('Geviert'), uniting earth and heaven and mortals and immortals. Heidegger refers to pre-modern examples and to romantic poems, but he also states that such a union has never existed and is yet to come. While arguing the need to overcome modern, Cartesian space making, and to rethink traditional place making, he refused the consolation of nostalgia. For designers he raised the question whether they can actually compose the cosmic unity he evoked. By de-framing the intimate court and re-framing it in the slightly uncanny follies (thus confronting the 'Heimlich' and the 'Unheimlich'), the project of Jan is able to 'make place' both for the ephemeral and for the everlasting, making indeed a place for the arts, and with architecture being one of them: for the art of framing escape.

conclusion

We have seen that a buitenplaats is both a monumental building and a valuable landscape, and that in order to deal with its heritage the question has to be raised how to frame a monument and how to frame a landscape. To give a sustainable future to a buitenplaats, a new use is required that earns the money to pay for its renovation and maintenance. The new use will not result in a form that follows functionalist logic. To account for the transformation of an existing form a different logic is needed. In this respect, the theory of representation offers insight in the role of the sign that mediates between the *reference* and the *concept*.

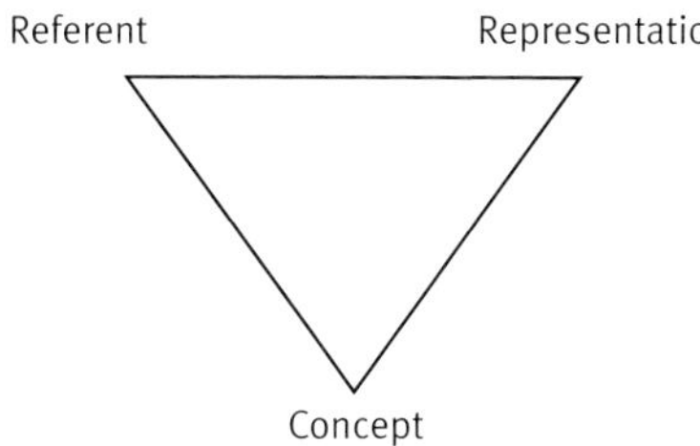

8. triangle of reference: 'toppled'

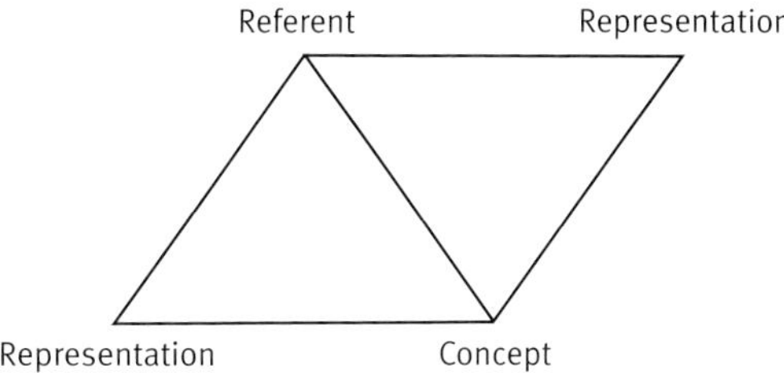

9. triangle of reference: 'truss'

The triangular diagram puts the concept on top and sign and reference at the base. In order to account for transformation it must be toppled so that the concept is the base: the initiator of a new relation between symbolic form and practical use (fig. 7). However, standing on its own this triangle would be too fragile. To remediate the instability, the two diagrams must be combined resulting in a stable truss that brings the three elements involved in the transformation into interaction (fig. 8).[7] According to me this combined diagram grasps the transformation operated by Jan Herwarts.

7. This is my interpretation of the diagram developed by
   Jos Bosman, in the conclusion of his doctoral dissertation
   'The Aura of Modernity - Architecture with a Broken Tradition',
   2005